D0870064

Future
Wave

Ed Hindson &
Lee Fredrickson

HARVEST HOUSE PUBLISHERS
Eugene, Oregon 97402

The Coming Wave

by Tim LaHaye, coauthor of
the bestselling *Left Behind* series

We are living in the most incredible times the world has ever known. Technological advances are taking place faster and faster, making what was once impossible become more and more commonplace.

A wave of technological innovation is sweeping the planet. This future wave is more than a simple wave that gently laps the shore. It is even more than a tidal wave that sweeps inland. It is a *tsunami* that swells up from the bowels of the ocean, moving with devastating speed across vast distances and wreaking havoc upon those who have clung to the seeming safety of the shore.

This book is a study of the technological phenomena that are sweeping the world today. Ed Hindson and Lee Fredrickson examine the unbelievable changes that technology is bringing to our society with two things in mind: First, they want to introduce you to the world of scientific and technological advances and challenge you to consider how these might be used to advance the work of God in the days ahead. And second, they want to raise words of caution and

7

warning about the potential dangers of a technologically dependent society and how its implements could play a part in the Antichrist's work in the days ahead.

The future wave has already begun. We cannot stop it. The question is should we ride it or run from it? The writers' response is that we should ride it! We believe that we as Christians need not fear the innovations of technology. Rather, we should use them to spread the gospel while there is still time. God has given human beings the intelligence we have so that we can develop technologies that can benefit our health, our education, and even our spiritual well-being.

The wave of new technologies also possesses a challenge to our generation. We dare not embrace technology naively or uncritically. We need to beware of the potential to become the victims of our own success. A technologically dependent society can easily become a society that no longer thinks for itself. For example, the longer we use calculators, the fewer people we will have who can carry out mathematical exercises without technological assistance. We are fully aware of the dangers this poses for the next generation.

The future wave, like a great *tsunami*, will carry everything in its path to greater heights in the days ahead. But eventually, like the *tsunami*, it will crash violently. We believe that technology will both benefit our lives and ensnare us at the same time, but we do not believe the crash will come until the Tribulation period, when the Antichrist will use some of this technology to control the world.

In the meantime, we have an opportunity to use a number of incredible innovations that make it possible for us to evangelize the entire world in our lifetime. Beyond that, the destructive force of technology looms on the horizon as well. In religious circles, most people recognize this dichotomy. But what about the millennium, the 1,000-year kingdom of God on earth after the Tribulation? Will God allow us to continue using technology for the good of humankind during the reign of Christ on earth? These are the issues that are raised—and endeavored to answer—in *Future Wave*. It is our prayer that through this book, God will challenge your thinking about the future and what it will really be like.

In *Future Wave*, Ed and Lee have combined biblical prophecies with futurist studies in order to project a picture of what the future might be like in light of the technologies that will be developed in the years ahead. They are especially grateful to Farris Robertson for his creative insights, editorial assistance, and leading-edge technological expertise. We believe that we are standing on the precipice of a whole new era in relation to understanding the biblical prophecies of the end times. May God give us the grace to serve Him faithfully in the days ahead.

—*Tim LaHaye*

1

Understanding the Wave

Future Wave

[Enter Story]

Waking Up in the Millennial Kingdom

A gentle ring wakes you up in the morning. Your eyes open to a wall-sized television screen showing the Temple in Jerusalem. The Temple was built by the Jews to exact specifications given to them by their Messiah, Jesus. A slow-moving waterway, lined with exotic trees, proceeds out of the Temple, passes through the priests' portion, into the outer court, some ten miles long, and continues through the countryside until it empties into the Living Sea, once called the Dead Sea.

Today, as always, there are worship songs emanating from the outer court as the Temple singers offer their songs of praise to King Jesus. Billions of people are watching with you as Jesus enters the court and addresses the world. At the conclusion of the address, a warm, friendly face you have named Holly replaces the Temple scene, cheerily announcing, "It's time to get out of bed and start your day."

Walking into the kitchen, the appliances sense your presence. The coffeepot turns itself on. Bread is toasted to the setting you prefer. Your favorite worship music gently fills the air. The intelligent house is now coming to life. Your day is just beginning in the first century of the millennial kingdom.

On the coffee table, Holly—your artificial intelligence agent—has prepared your personalized edition of the newspaper by scanning the global spiritual brain (once called the Internet). The sheet of digital paper changes as you touch the corner. The headline reads, "The last known case of cancer is finally eradicated and the world is officially cancer-free." As you leave the kitchen, the refrigerator scans its contents, and announces, "You're out of milk. And the yogurt is sour." Holly adds: "We're low on computers. Shall I have a dozen more delivered with your grocery order?"

Most of your friends have bought "intelligent agent" programs without faces or personalities. Some claim they get in the way; others prefer not to speak to their appliances. But you like the convenience of voice commands.

Before you leave, you instruct the robot vacuum cleaner to vacuum the carpet. It springs to life and, getting information from the GPS tracking device in the ceiling, begins its job cautiously and efficiently, while you get ready for the day.

To be continued. . .

The Future Thinker

Sound incredible? This is the future of life on planet earth in a world ruled by our Lord and Savior Jesus Christ. The story, with the artificial intelligence agent "Holly" as the main character, may sound more like science fiction, but, in fact, it is based on technology that is already being developed today. A number of ideas went into the creating of this story that are meant more for enjoyment than anything else. The same and similar ideas can be used in every area of your life and will better prepare you for the future. You too can be a "future thinker"!

When asked, "What do you worry about most on your job?" an executive responsible for the future development of a very large corporation gave this startling answer: "I worry most about what my people don't know they don't know. What they know they don't know, they're able to work on and find the answer to. But they can't do that if they don't know that they don't know!"

Today, most people go through life missing out on incredible opportunities for shaping their future simply because they don't know that they don't know. Their plans for the future are based on forecasts that get frozen into family budgets and day-to-day living. All too often they assume that the environment in which they live is either unchanging or boringly predictable.

Most people assume a future plan that validates their view of the future. This concept dominates their decision-making. This is the future they plan on without any way of guaranteeing it will come to pass. Futurists call this the "default scenario." It is usually based on some form of forecast or prediction based on our present experiences.

This would be fine if these forecasts held true, but we live in a world increasingly shaped by unknown factors and sudden changes. Uncertainty plagues the future so that our plans do not hold up to the stream of real events. This failure of strategic plans does not mean that strategy and planning are invalid; rather, it means we have to create a new approach to strategy and planning that takes into account the uncertainties of the future. We have to develop a strategy for the future that is based on the certainty of God's prophetic truth.

God and the Future

God has predetermined certain events in the future. These events are critical to prophetic teaching; they will not be changed. There will be a rapture of the church followed by a time of great tribulation on the earth that will last seven years (Daniel 9:24-27). This seven-year period will be followed by a time of utopia on this earth that will last 1,000 years (Revelation 20:1-6). We do not know the exact time of Christ's return, but it is clearly known to God. Jesus said, "No one knows about that day or hour, not even the angels in heaven...but only the Father" (Matthew 24:36).

God has already predetermined the exact second that those who have accepted Christ as Savior will be taken from this earth at the rapture. Those Christians who have died over the centuries will be resurrected, and those who are living on earth at that time will be raptured up together to meet the Lord in the air (1 Thessalonians 4:13-17).

Keeping in Mind the Will of God

Those who are without Christ sometimes try to create a future scenario based on the little they are able to determine of their own destiny. The Christian, by contrast, endeavors to find out the will of God and then cooperates with that will, to determine his future on this earth as well as his future in heaven. We are partners with God in this fast-paced world. Sometimes we may feel life would be easier if we said, "I've had enough! I'm getting off this roller coaster of life and I'm going to take it easy for a change." Satan would like for Christians to be passive and not get involved in serving God in this life or in the life to come. But we are missing out on a lot when we do that. We'll know fulfillment—and anticipate the future more—when we seek to do God's will. This will is revealed in the principles of His Word. Find His will for your life, and do it by His grace and to His glory.

Developing Flexible Strategies for the Future

A close study of the Scriptures shows us that God has alternate futures that are set before His people. How you see these alternate futures will determine your effectiveness in reaching a lost and dying world. What God said well over 2,000 years ago is still true today:

> If my people, who are called by my name, will humble themselves and pray and seek my face and turn from their wicked ways, then will I hear from heaven and will forgive their sin and will heal their land (2 Chronicles 7:14).

That word "if" should speak loudly to us. That word is saying that we have choices before us. God has a future for us. We can either ride the future wave, or we can let the future wave engulf us and carry us away into the deluge of technological advancement, preventing us from serving God effectively in the days ahead.

What Is Future Thinking?

Becoming a future thinker is like making the jump from a ballistic artillery shell to a guided heat-seeking missile. The artillery shell stays on one course to reach its target, while the guided heat-seeking missile pursues its target by moving one direction and then another before it finally reaches its destination.

In a fluid environment, there are many possible futures. It is somewhat like the weather, which can bring sunshine, rain, or snow. A future thinker embraces "what if?" questions that go outside the reach of his habitual mindset. This requires him to think with multiple futures in mind. Each "what if" question requires a different scenario of what might be. Each story will be equally plausible if we can come to a conclusion. All will challenge the assumptions upon which our "default scenario" is based. *Prophetic scenarios*, therefore, are Christ-centered views of the future that are consistent with the Bible and plausible with reality.

Constructing these different views of the future is not as easy as it first looks. This is because our view of the future is limited by our yielding to God's will. Our mindset is the view we have placed on the outside world, and is sustained through our belief system. This pattern is very hard to change. Some call this mindset a "paradigm"—a way of viewing reality. Our mindset sometimes will hold us to a default scenario and keep us from God's best. Here's an example we've created for this book:

A Man Stuck in Default Mode: Flashback to A.D. 31

A young affluent man came to Jesus one day with a question: "Good teacher, what must I do to inherit eternal life?"

(Luke 18:18). Jesus, who could see right into the heart of the man, knew his mindset. He challenged him with the Ten Commandments of the Law. "You know the commandments," Jesus replied. When the young man insisted he had kept the commandments—including loving God and loving his neighbor—Jesus told him, "You still lack one thing. Sell everything you have and give to the poor" (verse 22). Jesus was offering him more riches than the wealth of the whole world and an eternal life to enjoy it. But when the young man heard this challenge to his traditional thinking, he went away sad "because he was a man of great wealth" (verse 23).

After watching this man turn and walk away, Peter, the spokesman for the disciples, said to Jesus, "We have left all we had to follow you" (verse 28). Jesus knew that His disciples would receive the treasures of heaven that were offered to the rich young man, so He offered them a glimpse into the future. What He told them gives us information of future events that we can use to understand our future as well: "I tell you the truth, at the renewal of all things [the millennial reign of Christ], when the Son of Man sits on his glorious throne, you who have followed me will also sit on twelve thrones, judging the twelve tribes of Israel. And everyone who has left houses or brothers or sisters or father or mother or children or fields for my sake will receive a hundred times as much and will inherit eternal life" (Matthew 19:28-29).

In order to break out of our mindset (or paradigm) we must use imagination and logic to imagine the future.

Underlying this must be an understanding of the driving forces that are likely to be shaping the future. God is in control, and is determining the unfolding drama of this world, bringing events to pass that have caused many futurists to rethink their concepts of the future.

The Bible is the Biblical Futurist's Textbook

The Interpretation of Bible Prophecy

Without an accurate understanding of what the Bible says about future events, we cannot hope to have a view of the future that lines up with God's timetable.

When studying the Bible, a consistent literal interpretation of the text is essential to properly understanding what God is saying. Literal interpretation involves an approach that is based on the ordinary meaning of the actual words, and refraining from going beyond the facts into wild speculation. In its simplest form, literal interpretation means to explain the original sense of the Bible according to the normal and customary usage of the words in the text.

Literal interpretation recognizes that a word or phrase can be used either plainly or figuratively. A "golden rule of interpretation" has been developed to help us discern whether or not the author intended a figure of speech. This rule is often expressed like this: When the plain sense of Scripture makes common sense, seek no other sense; therefore, take every word at its primary, ordinary, usual, literal meaning unless the facts of the immediate context, studied in the light of related passages and fundamental truths, indicate clearly otherwise.

This means that the prophetic portions of the Bible are interpreted in the same way as any other portion. The prophetic sections of the Bible use the same conventions of language found elsewhere in the Bible. A simplified form of the rule of literal interpretation goes like this: If the literal sense makes good sense, seek no other sense lest you arrive at nonsense!

Four Different Views of the Future

There are four differing views in relation to time—past, present, future, and timeless—that have been adopted by Christians to explain the future.

The *preterist* view believes that most, if not all, prophecy has already been fulfilled in the past—usually in relation to the destruction of Jerusalem in A.D. 70. They view the fall of Jerusalem to the Roman army as the "second coming" of Christ.

The *historicist* view sees much of the current church age as equal to the Tribulation period. It sees all prophecy as being fulfilled during the church age. Thus, current events are often paralleled to future predictions. Everything from the fall of Rome to World War II is viewed as being prophesied in Scripture.

The *futurist* view believes that virtually all prophetic events will not occur in the current church age, but will happen in the future during the tribulation, second coming, or millennial reign of Christ on earth. This view believes in a literal rapture, return, tribulation, and millennium in the future.

The *idealist* view is timeless. The idealist does not believe that the Bible indicates the timing of events; therefore, we cannot know anything before it happens. Idealist thinking takes prophetic passages and places them in the context of teaching great ideas or truths about God that are to be applied to our lives regardless of timing.

This book holds to a futurist perspective; we believe that the tribulation period and the millennial reign of Christ will follow the rapture of the church on earth.

Your Brain Has a Future Zone

Human intelligence and the structure of the brain are set up to deal with future uncertainties. Our brain has a zone dedicated to dealing with the future; it forms a "memory" of the future. In a healthy individual, this part of the brain is rehearsing and storing many images of possible futures; "If this happens, then I will do that." In an individual with certain mental difficulties, there is only one memory of the future and so when this future does not come to pass the person suffers a breakdown. The expectations are brittle and the capacity to respond to change is poor. This single view of the future, whether it is a forecast or an expectation of continuity of the present, is referred to as the default scenario.

Peter Schwartz, in his book *The Art of the Long View,* says, "Using scenarios is rehearsing the future. You run through the simulated events as if you were already living them. You train yourself to recognize which drama is unfolding. That helps you avoid unpleasant surprises, and know how to act."[1]

When you go on a journey, such as a hike in the mountains, you may be planning on fine weather. As you consider the route and conditions and you pack your provisions and equipment, you ask yourself, *What if a mist descends? What if it snows? What if I sprain an ankle? What if I get delayed a day and have to bivouac?* These mental rehearsals may change the equipment you take and lead you to think about alternative routes. These rehearsals will also make you think about the personal skills you'll need for dealing with contingencies. Armed with these memories of the future, you are much better prepared to cope with whatever might happen during your journey.

Taking a Look at the Future

If the future is so uncertain, isn't writing scenarios about it rather speculative, like science fiction? This is not the case if we understand that developing scenarios of the future can begin from becoming more aware of what is going on right now. To build plausible scenarios of the future, we need to cultivate a range of perceptions much wider than our customary one.

For example, learning from the past can help us to project the future. Also, there are always pockets of the future in the present. Some countries do things today that will take five or ten years to reach other countries. Some sectors of society are right now living in a way that is our future. Some people have ideas that will take 20 years to incubate and become generally accepted. Technologies already exist that people have not yet heard of that will one day be commonplace.

As we think about the prophetic future, we must begin to see the future through very different eyes. One way this is done is to gain access to and interview people who have very special perceptions about what is happening today and what will happen in the future.

The Future of the Internet

When asked about the future of the Internet, Dr. James Hendler, a computer expert, believes that the Web will have artificial intelligence. He tells us:

> I think the biggest change in artificial intelligence
> will be scaling it to the Internet and solving some of
> the big problems the net has. Right now when you
> do a search on the Web, it's hard to do with

meaning. The artificial intelligence community has been studying that problem for a long time, mostly on fairly small, very specific problems. We've created a lot of technology that is starting to move to that kind of Web, so I think you'll see a lot of that work soon—much smarter Web searches, much better Web agents.

In fact, I think agents will be the things you'll see after that. Probably 10 to 15 years from now, I'm guessing, your interaction with the Internet will be much like your interaction with the world when you go on a trip.

You'll have personal helpers who will help you find your content, deal with the pages. Right now when you go to get something on the Web, you have to figure out which information has to go where and how to specify it, and [whether] they mail it or e-mail it and what addresses to put where. All of that should be automatic, and should be done for you—much the way your travel agent books your ticket.[2]

The Future of Language

Through his work at the University of Southern California, Dr. Eduard Hovy is exploring the future of language—and how computers will help tear down the Tower of Babel that still divides much of mankind. He also predicts machines will help us understand still-incomprehensible dead languages, as well as communicate with those with whom we have never communicated before. He writes:

> In the very long term, language will disappear into the computer and become intimately tied with its internal representations of the world, of meaning, of everything. In the short term, we'll see lots of little spinoffs of this: applications that understand you—

smart rooms, smart clothes—you speak to your car, you speak to your whatever. These things will help you live in the world and will teach you and find information for you and do things for you. But the core theme will be creating understanding, creating real knowledge in a machine. For me, language is a window into this, much easier than some of the other ways people try building meaning.[3]

On the evolution of a global language, Dr. Hovy writes this:

If you look at history, people like to break off sub-languages, and dialects evolve. And as languages get older, they become more complex and more varied. So because we have this very big interconnection today through the Web and e-mail, there is a force toward one or two global macro-languages.

But I think that as soon as computers are able to translate well enough, you'll always have a choice: Do I write in my home language and trust the computer to translate it into the other 7,000 languages? Or do I try to write in the inter-lingua—let's say it's English—and don't express myself so well, and hope that other people, who also don't read it so well, will read it well enough.

If you look at how many new Web pages are coming online every day, and at the addition of new languages, before 2003 English is going to be used by less than 50 percent of the world's people. It's still going to be the single biggest one, but less than half.[4]

On man's ability to translate languages, Dr. Hovy writes this:

People are trying to create automatic translation systems. Say you take the Canadian parliamentary records, which are parallel French and English—or you take the Hong Kong parliamentary records, which are parallel Chinese and English—and you tell the system, "learn." And it learns which words go with which words, statistically, and learns the orders of the words and things.

The people building these translation engines don't say, "I'm doing translation." They say, "I have English and I have some kind of coded, mysterious form of English. And so I have to learn to decode the coded form—whether it's French or Chinese, I don't care."

The very latest thing was done over the summer [1999]. People built a system to learn Chinese-to-English translations in 24 hours. That's never been done. When you put in an arbitrary Chinese sentence, the output is fairly crude—only about half the time it's correct. But it's never been done this quickly![5]

Dr. Hovy has this to say about computer linguistics helping with education:

There's no point in going to a library and looking through 17 books and realizing, "I can't read all these books in the next five days before I must give my homework assignment in." But what if you could have a thing help you pull out the main pieces and structure them for you and present them for you and give you the links? Click here, and it tells you to look in this book, page 15, paragraph three. A dynamic tutor. Any topic you want. And you can go and explore to whatever depth you need.

This is great for kids, right? It means they don't have to do much work. But, it's a challenge for teachers, who ask, "Once you've got this, how do I test that you, the kid, have internalized this stuff?" That's a hard piece. I don't know how to solve that.

But I have no doubt language engines like these are going to exist and be used by business people who want to scope out a new market, by anybody who wants to learn anything, by the intelligence agencies who want to monitor what is happening in Pakistan or Bangladesh or somewhere.[6]

The Future of Space Travel

Will humankind ever travel to the galaxies of distant stars? Alex Roland thinks so. But the former NASA historian and History Department chair at Duke University believes space travel and exploration will come into its own only after some significant technological breakthroughs—and when such travel and exploration becomes lucrative.

For the next 20 to 30 years, I'm quite sure we're going to see no difference whatsoever. We're going to have more of what we've had for the last 30 to 40 years, which is, at considerable risk and great expense, sending humans up into low orbit—who float around and look busy and come back to Earth—and not really accomplishing very much. And it will continue to be the case during this period of the next 20 to 30 years that automated spacecraft will perform the most useful functions in space, and make the most important discoveries.

One thing that could change that, sometime in the next century, is...a dramatic technological break-through in launch vehicle development, which will allow us to get off the surface of the Earth much more efficiently and much more safely than we can now. And once we can put people and more sup-plies and equipment and cargo in Earth orbit more effectively than we do now, then that will open up space in a way that's simply not available to us now.

One other set of activities might make that happen even without a technological breakthrough—war and commerce. If we discovered a large-scale commercial enterprise in space that paid for itself—then we might see large-scale space activity, and humans could go into space as part of the infrastructure.[7]

Roland also offers these thoughts about what represents the future of space technology:

I would expect it's probably *nanotechnology*. That is, attempts to build computers and machines at virtually the atomic level, so that a very small package can prove to be a very powerful instrument in space— not just a passive scientific instrument receiving information, but an actual machine that can do work out in space. And if that technology proceeds in the way it now seems to, we will be able to send very powerful instruments very long distances at very high rates of speed. Also, we can put very, very powerful instruments up into low Earth orbit at very slight cost. That has enormous commercial implications.[8]

The Future of Books

Will we still turn pages in 2010?

Computer screens can now show words as sharply as they appear on the printed page. Books, magazines, and newspapers will be able to be routinely read on screens or in formats that are the size of small books.

The clash of the book culture and the e-book culture may be all but over in the year 2010. On the one side of this clash we have the people of the book. They love the smell of books. They love to curl up in a cozy chair with their favorite coffee and lose themselves in the printed page. They live by the book. They respect the authority derived from the author. The foundation for their life is ultimately housed in texts, and they are all on the same page.

On the other side are the people of the screen. They are the people who, at the extreme, have a screen in their living room, kitchen, bathroom, bedroom, ceiling, and mailbox. These screens are in the form of TV screens, computer screens, telephone screens, cell-phone screens, and screens that we can only imagine today. Their world flies by them in sound bites, computer bytes, and screen pixels. On their screens, words can move from right to left or left to right, and can morph into pictures, and can change colors. The people of the page and the people of the screen will finally come together on common ground when electronic ink is introduced.

The ink itself is a liquid that can be printed onto nearly any surface. Within the liquid are millions of tiny microcapsules, each one containing white particles suspended in a dark dye. When an electric field is applied, the white particles move to one end of the microcapsule, where they become visible. This makes the surface appear white at that spot. An opposite electric field pulls the particles to the other end of the microcapsules, where they are hidden by the dye. This makes the surface appear dark at that spot.

This electronic paper looks and feels just like real paper printed with real ink, except the ink on the electronic paper can change, much like the characters on a computer screen can change.

Bind 400 pages of e-paper coated with e-ink, and you have a true e-book. It looks and feels and is read exactly like any book in the library. But when you're done reading it, you can plug it into a phone line or a wireless receiver and change the entire content of the book.

The ink also has a very low power usage. On top of that, a user can receive news, display it on the page and switch off the power source. The ink retains the image for weeks without the need of additional power. What's more, because the ink can be attached to a sheet of paper, printed materials using this ink will weigh the same as newspapers today. And, as is the case with many electronic devices, sunlight would not be an enemy. The e-ink display will be just as easy or easier to read in sunlight.

Jim Sachs, founder and CEO of SoftBook Press, recently said:

> In the future, eBooks will take advantage of all the important trends in computing devices—such as display technology, microelectronics, connectivity options and more; but most importantly, they will be optimized for a simple, pleasurable reading experience. While there will many types of eBook readers, most will be designed not for the current 2% of the world's population that owns a computer, but for the majority of people who can simply read.
>
> In 20 years, eBooks readers will be wireless and connected to a multitude of bookstores and libraries on the Internet, providing immediate access to virtually every book ever written. Magazines and newspapers will be delivered directly to eBook readers wherever they are, allowing subscribers to purchase goods and services directly from advertisers with a simple click. eBook readers will be universally used in education, eliminating the 40-pound backpack, and dramatically improving a student's ability to consume, organize, interact [with] and retain information.

Like home videos, digital music, and interactive media, the emergence of eBook technology will enable new creative and business opportunities for artists. Interactive novels, electronic serials, short-form works, real-time updates to scientific and current event subjects, and other new forms of content we can't begin to imagine are all enabled by the emergence of the eBook.

And what about the time-honored, contemplative and enriching role that reading has had upon our lives for hundreds of years? Will it be sacrificed to the frenetic, fleeting and mass-consumption qualities that seem to distinguish Web content from traditional books? To that, we say it is not the medium that contributes to the quality of an author's work, but the words that form, shape and illuminate great ideas. Be assured, eBooks are the future of reading.[9]

The convenience and advantages of electronic devices will finally be married to all the reasons readers have loved paper books, magazines, and newspapers for centuries. The future will combine the best of both. And suppose that by the year 2015, we receive a newsflash that reads, "Reliable simultaneous language translation has been cracked with immediate consequences for the multilingual world"? Such an achievement would have far-reaching effects in the world as we know it.

What Does This Tell Us?

What do the futures of the Internet, language, space travel, and books have to do with *our* future? Each one of these futures, and the myriad of other futures that we will look at, give us a picture of our future and the future of mankind as it relates to God's timetable. Each builds on the other until we can create a story that takes place in the:

- *Near-Term Future:* up to one year from now

- *Short-Range Future:* one to five years from now

- *Middle-Range Future:* five to 20 years from now

- *Long-Range Future:* 20 to 50 years from now

- *Far Future:* 50-plus years from now

Most individuals, as well as most businesses and governments, only look ahead about four to five years in their planning (in politics usually until the next election, and in business, usually up to the next five years). It is important to look further ahead, however, in a world undergoing the rapid changes we are experiencing today. Our present-day activities are creating the world that we'll be living in about five to 20 years from now (the Middle-Range Future). Almost anything can be created—if we have a vision of what we want to create and are also personally committed to making that vision a reality in the future.

It is also important to remember that while the past, the present, and the future are all somehow interconnected, the only place from which to change the future is in the *now.* The power for change resides in the present moment, for that is the only place from which our thoughts or actions can actually bring about change.

There is no mechanical way to use these components to assemble scenarios. They are created through a combination of research, analysis, hard thinking, and imagination. They involve the skills of the storyteller as well as the strategist.

Thinking about the future is often difficult for Christians. On the one hand, we know the Bible predicts the devastation of the planet during the tribulation period. On the other hand, it also predicts the transcendent glory of the eternal state—the new heaven and the new earth. What most of us forget is the 1,000-year millennial kingdom of Christ on earth that occurs between these two future realities. God has a wonderful future planned for this planet that will last for 1,000 years, and we will be here to enjoy it.

2

The Future Is Now

How are we to react to the comforts, companionship, sense of power, and pleasure—both physical and mental—that technology brings to our lives? With the exponential advances that this technowave is bringing to the planet it would be easy for our human spirit to become impersonalized as being online in virtual reality and cyberspace takes the place of being inline with God.

For most of us, technology is far from neutral. It shapes our choices and directs our actions. Some people automatically turn to technology for a solution rather than turning to God. Others never turn to technology for a solution, but rather have drawn a line in the sand and vow never to cross. Some of us have a relationship with technology and God that rebounds from one extreme to the other. One moment we are afraid of it and draw close to God, the next moment we are inspired by the power it gives us and draw away from God. In this chapter, we are going to examine how people relate to technology, which includes, to some degree, elements of both fear and worship.

Though at first glance technology and theology might appear to be poles apart, a strong connection has actually been present throughout history. Christian futurists, since the time of Augustine, have addressed issues of science and technology. These theologians recognized the importance of understanding the advances brought on by technology and putting these advances in a biblical perspective.

One area of concern to Christians is the hope that individuals and society as a whole have placed in technology. Indeed, for some, technology has become a false god of hope, a path that will lead them into becoming their own gods. For these people the future will be a technological paradise. These dreamers see a future world where machines replace men and women in the work force, creating a near-workerless society of abundance and leisure.

Advanced Automatons: Year 2020

By the year 2020 advanced automatons are a fixture of everyday life. Until recently the primitive versions of these automatons were just used in the industrial sector of life. They were preprogrammed or remote-controlled. They were first seen at places like Danbury Hospital, where Help-Mate, a four-foot medical robot, was used to fetch drugs and equipment for doctors and nurses, following a map of the hospital lodged in its memory. It was operated by punching commands on a keyboard. And then there was Sentry, a 485-pound robot that acted as a security guard.

Moving along at five miles per hour, it worked fine and even thwarted a burglary at Boston's Bayside Exposition Center.

The second-generation automatons popped up around 2010. They proved to be reliable helpers, able to navigate in factories, hospitals, and homes and perform well-defined functions. These were called Volks-robots. They mowed the lawn, acted as butlers, even performed car tune-ups, and you can't forget those gourmet meals they cooked up for that night alone with the two of you and, of course, with your Volks-robot.

The third generation showed up around 2020. These Robo-Droids could now learn from their mistakes. Although they were clumsy at first, they learned from their constant interaction with humans. Some think that the Robo-Droids seem to feel pain and pleasure via a system programmed into them that would reinforce certain positive acts and prohibit negative ones.

Is technology a tool to make life more comfortable? A toy to make life happier? Or a tyrant that molds us into a reality we don't want?

From a biblical perspective, technology falls under a mandate given to Adam and Eve in the Garden. Theologians refer to this mandate as the *cultural mandate:*

> God said, "Let us make man in our image, in our likeness, and let them rule over the fish of the sea and the birds of the air, over the livestock, over all the earth, and over all the creatures that move along

the ground." So God created man in his own image, in the image of God created he him; male and female created he them. God blessed them, and said to them, "Be fruitful and increase in number; fill the earth and subdue it. Rule over the fish of the sea and the birds of the air and over every living creature that moves on the ground" (Genesis 1:26-28).

Science and technology originate from an understanding of and interaction with creation. With regard to technology and the cultural mandate, Stephen Monsma wrote:

> Christian theologians have initiated few systematic reflections on modern technology. Indeed, Christians have often not seriously concerned themselves with either the negative or the positive consequences of modern scientific-technological development. They have viewed technology either as something that is naturally good or as a development that is neutral in relation to the Christian faith.[1]

The neglect of Christians in addressing technology from a theological perspective has resulted in secularism's view of technology being predominant in our society. When users and developers of technology accept secularism's view uncritically, there is a tendency to develop the technology toward the dark side instead of light. How should we as Christians respond to the advances in technology, and where should we exert major efforts?

Technology Is an Instrument of Power

We (Ed and Lee) are proponents of this view and "hold that technology is neither inherently good nor inherently evil but is an ambiguous instrument of power whose consequences depend on its social context."[2] While technology itself is amoral, we must still consider technology in the context of the intentions of the inventor, and in some cases even the users. We can say that technology is not wholly neutral because the origin of each technology discussed in this book can be traced back to its inventor or discoverer, and in each case, we can find ethical decisions of consequence that were made in that technology's developments.

Ian Barbour writes of the relationship of this position to Christianity:

> This position seems to me more consistent with the biblical outlook than either of the alternatives. Preoccupation with technology does become a form of idolatry, a denial of the sovereignty of God, and a threat to distinctively human existence. But technology directed to genuine human needs is a legitimate expression of humankind's creative capacities and an essential contribution to its welfare.[3]

Figuring Out the Future of Technology

Because technology is still a very new field, it is still possible to see how all the pieces that began in the twentieth century could fall into place in the twenty-first century. It is also possible to construct a basic picture of the world of 2020 and beyond. At the same time, however, we are not prophets or predictors of the future. One of the problems with trying to predict the future is that by the time it's clear, the predictions have little resemblance to actual events. Then, of course, it's too late to get your money back.

Here are some examples of intelligent people who staked their reputation on predictions:

- "The telephone has too many shortcomings to be seriously considered as a means of communication."
  —Western Union executive, 1876

- "Airplanes have no military value."

    —Professor Marshal Foch, 1912

- "I think there is a world market for maybe five computers."

    —IBM Chairman Thomas Watson, 1943

- "It would appear that we have reached the limits of what is possible to achieve with computer technology, although one should be careful with such statements, as they tend to sound pretty silly in five years."

    —John von Neumann, 1949

- "640,000 bytes of memory ought to be enough for anybody."

    —Bill Gates, 1981

As for the contents of this book, we are not prophets. But what we're about to share is based on God's Word and the observation of a powerful wave in motion today. This wave began at the end of the military state of readiness in the 1980s, and has been marked by incredible new technologies, not the least of which is the Internet. The end of the Cold War also saw the triumph of a set of ideas long championed by the United States—those of the free-market economy and, to some extent, liberal democracy. This helped to clear the way for the creation of a truly global economy with one integrated market. Not just half of the world, the free world, but everybody on the planet in the same economy. This is historically unprecedented, with more unprecedented achievements to follow. In the 1990s, the United States experienced a booming economy. But looking ahead to the next decade, it may be true we haven't seen anything yet. We may be entering an unrelenting economic expansion, a truly global economic wave. We call it the *future wave*.

The Five Great Technowaves of the Future

The basic science is now in place for five great technowaves:

- personal computers
- telecommunications
- biotechnology
- nanotechnology
- alternative energy

These technologies will greatly enhance the church's ability to evangelize the world. The rise of Asia as a bastion of power, for example, simply can't be stopped. This is not to say that there aren't some huge unknowns, the critical uncertainties, such as how the United States handles its key role as world leader.

Why do we paint a positive scenario of the future? During the global standoff of the Cold War, society was clinging to a scenario that too often amounted to little more than surviving a nuclear war. Some called this MAD (mutually assured destruction). Today, without the old visions of the last millennium and new visions for a future world, it is easy to see how these five great technowaves could all surge together into something better. But without an open vision of the future, people tend to get shortsighted, looking out only for themselves. A positive scenario can inspire us through what will inevitably be traumatic times ahead when the great wave comes crashing down, but we don't want to tell the end of the story just quite yet.

With the Waves Come Responsibility

We are not saying that the church should not warn the wicked world of the consequences of rejecting God. Like the prophet Ezekiel, we must blow the trumpet and warn the world of a coming sword upon the land (Ezekiel 33:1-11).

The spiritual vacuum of our times is being filled with the darkness of evil. We are no longer a predominantly Christian society. The symbols and trappings of Christianity remain, but the heart and soul of it have been polluted by the secular pursuit of life without God. More and more, it is evident that the majority of people are looking in all the wrong places to find meaning and purpose for their lives.

Aleksandr Solzhenitsyn has remarked, "The forces of evil have begun their decisive offensive." So it seems that we are digging in for what may well be the final onslaught against biblical Christianity. The final blow may not come from a direct offensive of anti-Christian sentiment, but from sheer neglect of its message. After all, what better way to undermine the gospel than to live as though it did not exist?

We see evidence of that neglect in every form of art, music, literature, and film. Many of today's artists and writers are void of spiritual values, conflicts, and concerns. They are so ignorant of biblical truth that they go about their lives as if there were no God. Movies are full of characters like the one portrayed by Michael Douglas in *Wall Street*, who bellows out: "Greed is good! Greed works!" Then there is the proverbial prostitute characterized by Julia Roberts in *Pretty Woman*, who defends her profession with the inane remark, "You gotta make a living."

These are just a few of the many examples of non-Christian or even anti-Christian sentiments that prevail in modern culture. It's true that there are still many believers who have not capitulated to secularism, materialism, and pragmatism, but all too often, these attitudes can be found even within the Christian community. It is as though the darkness is so great that even we as Christians can't always find our way through the maze of modern life.

We have every convenience conceivable to make our lives easier. Jet airplanes speed us across the country and around the world in a matter of hours. Satellite television transmissions bring world events to us within seconds. Air conditioning cools us in the summer; central heating warms us in the winter. For many, life is no longer a struggle for raw survival. It is often the pursuit of life, liberty, and happiness, just as America's forefathers planned.

But the freedom to pursue life often allows us to become sidetracked from its true meaning and purpose. Many of us are so busy these days that we can't sit still long enough to enjoy the life we have. Most of us overextend and overcommit ourselves to the point that even our leisure time increases our stress level.

The New Dark Ages?

Charles Colson has noted that the church had to stand alone against the barbarian culture of the Dark Ages.[4] Classical Rome had become corrupt from within and fell to the waves of warring bands of illiterate barbarian tribes. Medieval Europe lay in the shambles of spiritual darkness, but the church fought illiteracy, moral degradation, and political corruption. The barbarians could not withstand the stubborn resistance of Christian civilization. In time, Europe emerged from the Dark Ages into an era of spiritual and intellectual creativity and growth.

Colson sees the church at a similar crisis point today—confronting the new Dark Ages. The Bible predicts that a time of spiritual apostasy will precede the revealing of the Antichrist ("the man of sin" in 2 Thessalonians 2:3). The book of Revelation describes this apostasy as the religion of the "great whore." She is the epitome of false religion and spiritual adultery. By contrast, the New Testament church is pictured as a virgin betrothed to Christ.

Spiritual confusion is already paving the way for technology to fill the spiritual vacuum in our lives. While technology is amoral—that is, it is neither good nor evil—it can be used for both good and evil purposes. Yet the potential for evil should not lead us to overlook the tremendous benefits of technology. Nor should technology's benefits cause us to accept its consequences blindly.

Isn't it interesting to note that we have more conveniences, more technology, and more leisure time than any society has ever had, and yet most people today are not happy? When will we learn that things will not make us happy? Only God can satisfy the human heart's longing for true joy and happiness. Jesus said, "I have come that they may have life, and have it to the full" (John 10:10).

Our generation must face the fact that life works only when it is lived God's way. As long as we continue seeking the meaning and purpose of life without God, we will never find it. Only when men and women come to the end of themselves and turn to God will they find the true meaning of life.

3

The Computer Wave

In order to see the future, we must look at it from a historical vantage point. Around 1980, two developments started that would have profound consequences for the U.S. economy, the Western economy, and then the global economy at large. One was the introduction of personal computers. The other was the breakup of the Bell System. These events triggered two of the five great technowaves that are helping to fuel the future wave.

The Driving Force Behind the Computer Wave

As we consider the sweep of technological history, it is worthwhile to note Moore's law, which describes an interesting principle regarding the entire computer revolution. Moore's law states that computing speeds and densities double every 18 months. In other words, every 18 months we can buy a computer that is twice as fast and has twice as much memory for the same cost. Remarkably, this law has held true for more than 100 years, from the mechanical card-based computing technology used for the 1890 census, to the relay-based computers of the 1940s, to the vacuum tube-based computers of the 1950s, to the transistor-based machines of the 1960s, to all of the generations of integrated circuits since. If you put every calculator and computer since 1890 on a logarithmic chart, you'll end up with an essentially straight line.

Computer memory, for example, is about 16,000 times more powerful for the same unit cost as it was 20 years ago. Computer memory is about 100 million times more powerful for the same unit cost as it was in 1948. If the automobile industry had made as much progress in the past 47 years, a car today would cost one-hundredth of a cent and would go faster than the speed of light.

Dr. Gordon Moore, who became Intel's CEO in 1975, first observed this phenomenon in the mid 1960s, at which time he said that the doubling occurred every 24 months. Ten years later, he revised this to 18 months. There are more than enough new computing technologies being developed to assure a continuation of Moore's law for a very long time.

Flashback 1940:
The Computer Wave Begins

By 1940 Hitler had the mainland of Europe in his grasp, and England was preparing for an anticipated invasion. The British government placed a high priority on the value of computation and organized its best mathematicians and electrical engineers, under the intellectual leadership of

Alan Turing, with the mission of cracking the German military code. The British recognized that with the German air force enjoying superiority in the skies, failure to accomplish this mission (code-named ULTRA) was likely to doom the nation. In order not to be distracted from their task, the group lived in the tranquil community of Dollis Hill, a suburb north of London, with a parallel effort at Bletchley Park, 40 miles northwest of London.

The British government had obtained a working model of the German "Enigma" coding machine in 1938 from a still-unheralded hero of World War II, a young Jewish Polish engineer named Richard Lewinsky, who had worked briefly in eastern Germany helping to assemble the device. Coded orders sent by radio from the German high command were easily intercepted, but to decode these messages, every combination of the positions of the Enigma machine's coding wheels needed to be evaluated. Turing and his colleagues constructed a series of machines in 1940 from telephone relays that they called "Robinson," after a popular cartoonist who drew "Rube Goldberg" machines. The group's own Rube Goldberg device succeeded brilliantly and provided the British with a transcription of nearly all significant Nazi messages.

As the Germans continued to add to the complexity of their code (by adding additional coding wheels to their Enigma coding machine), Turing and his associates replaced Robinson's electromagnetic intelligence (which took about three-tenths of a second to add two numbers) with an electronic version called Colossus, built in 1943 from 2,000 radio tubes. Colossus, which was 1,500 times faster than Robinson, and nine similar machines running in parallel, provided an uninterrupted decoding of vital military intelligence to the Allied war effort.

Use of this information required supreme acts of discipline on the part of the British government. When informed by ULTRA that Coventry was to be bombed, Churchill ordered that the city not be warned, and that no civil defense steps be taken, lest preparations arouse German suspicions that their code had been cracked. The information provided by Robinson (the world's first operational special-purpose computer) and Colossus was used only with the greatest discretion (for example, to guide critical British ships through the German U-boats), but the cracking of Enigma was enough to enable the Royal Air Force to win the Battle of Britain.

Fueled by the horrors of war, and drawing upon a diversity of intellectual traditions, a new form of intelligence emerged on Earth. Later, this form of intelligence would be called the computer. The similarity of the computational process to the human thinking process was not lost on Turing, and he is credited with having established much of the theoretical foundations of computation and the ability to apply this new technology to the emulation of intelligence. In his classic 1950 paper, "Computing Machinery and Intelligence," published in the journal *Mind*, Turing predicted that by early in the next century, society will simply take for granted the pervasive intervention of intelligent machines in all phases of life, and that "the use of words and general educated opinion will have altered so much that one will be able to speak of machines thinking without expecting to be contradicted."[1]

Computer Trends for the Future

In the 1950s and 1960s, progress came so rapidly that some of the early pioneers felt that mastering the functionality of the human brain might not be so difficult after all.

The full impact of computers on society came in the early 1980s, when personal computers were steadily adopted by more and more businesses. By 1990, they began to enter the home, and the microprocessor was being embedded in many other tools and products, such as cars. By the turn of the century, with the power of computer chips still doubling roughly every 18 months, everything comes with a small, cheap silicon brain. Tasks like handwriting recognition become a breeze.

In his book *Technofutures*, James Canton of technofutures.com outlines the top ten computer trends for the twenty-first century.[2]

1. Computers will become powerful extensions of human beings, designed to augment intelligence, learning, communications, and productivity.

2. Computers will become intuitive—they will "learn," "recognize," and "know" what we want, who we are, and even what we desire.

3. Computer chips will be everywhere, and they will become invisible—embedded in everything from brains and hearts, to clothes and toys.

4. Computers will manage essential global systems, such as transportation and food production, better than humans will.

5. Online computer resources will enable us to download applications on-demand via wireless access anywhere and anytime.

6. Computers will become voice-activated, networked, video-enabled, and connected together over the Internet, linked with each other and humans.

7. Computers will have digital senses—speech, sight, smell, and hearing—enabling them to communicate with humans and other machines.

8. Neural networks and other forms of artificial intelligence will make computers as smart as humans and smarter for certain jobs.

9. The evaluation of humans and computers will converge. Synthetic intelligence will greatly enhance the next generation of humans.

10. As computers surpass human intelligence, a new digital species and a new culture will evolve that is parallel to our own.

By 2010, we may very well be using portable computers as our primary source for information. Intel builds a chip with a billion transistors 100 times the complexity of the most advanced integrated circuits being designed in the late 1990s. These chips are housed in computers that are dramatically lighter and thinner than the notebook computers of ten years earlier. In fact, these computers are available in a wide range of sizes and shapes, and are commonly embedded in wristwatches, rings, earrings, and other body ornaments.

Instead of carrying one computer, there will be at least a dozen computers on and around your body, and possibly in your body in the form of biochip implants. These tiny computers are networked using wireless local-area networks. They will provide communication similar to cellular phones, pagers, and Web surfing devices. Their functions will include:

• monitoring your body (for health and medical purposes)

- provide for automated identity (for conducting financial transactions and allowing entry into secure areas)

- providing directions for navigation and transportation

In most cases, these miniature computers will have no moving parts. Memory will be completely electronic, and, in fact, most personal computers will no longer require keyboards, because they will be personalized to your voice. Cables are also disappearing; they are being replaced by short-distance wireless technology. The majority of the text placed on computers will be created using continuous speech recognition (CSR) dictation software. Digital files such as books, music, movies, and software can be rapidly distributed as data files through the wireless network.

Computers will be the digital brains of the twenty-first century. As computers become more powerful with increased memory capacity and growing intelligence, they will be able to do more than simply co-exist with humans. This intimate connection will allow us to create new lifestyles and will change the very nature of society and the way we do business. The world we live in will be totally different when we have a billion transistors on a chip, processing millions of transactions in the blink of an eye. Computers operating at the speed of thought will be commonplace. By 2010, the computers in our homes will perform about a trillion calculations per second, compared to 600 million in 2000. But the most significant breakthrough is the supercomputer, which is the fastest computer in the world.

The supercomputers in 2010 should be around 20,000 times more powerful than the personal computers of that day. This means that the supercomputers will be capable of performing about 20 million billion calculations per second, or two quadrillion. This, by the way, is a very significant number.

The Computing Power of the Brain

Ralph Merkle, a computer scientist at Xerox PARC, published a paper in 1989 evaluating the intellectual processing power of the human brain. He measured it in three different ways.[3]

Method One: There are about one quadrillion synapses in the brain. They process about ten nerve impulses per second. Therefore the brain carries out about ten quadrillion synapse operations per second.

Method Two: The human retina (which has its own processing power and is relatively well understood) contains about 100 million nerve cells performing about ten billion addition operations per second. The brain is bigger than the retina by a factor of somewhere between 100 and 10,000. Therefore the brain must process between one and 100 trillion operations per second.

Method Three: The human brain consumes about 25 watts of energy, of which about ten watts are used directly for mental processes. We know the power consumption of a single synapse and can estimate the average distance between synapses. This means we can figure the maximum number of synapse operations that can be supported by the brain's "power supply." The upper limit turns out to be two quadrillion-synapse operations per second.

So, the supercomputer will equal the processing power of the human brain. Will it be possible to create an info morph of a human brain in a computer? (That is, to create the capabilities of the human brain in a computer.) One problem that needs to be considered is memory. The human brain's memory capacity is enormous, since it stores many sights, sounds, and concepts going back to birth. How many bytes are needed to replicate it?

Merkle examined this question in another paper, published in 1994, which tackled the general problem of making an accurate copy of a human brain.[4] First, he asked how much physical detail is important. Do we need to know the position of every brain atom? No. Every molecule? Probably not. The contents of each synapse? Maybe. Research indicates that one bit of memory information is actually stored across thousands or even millions of synapses, but let's play it safe and say it is stored in all of them.

According to Merkle, if each synapse is described by one byte and there are one quadrillion synapses, then we'll need a memory of one quadrillion bytes. In terms of computer memory, it would take one million gigabytes to reach one quadrillion bytes. With the cost of storage going down and the capacities of hard drives continuing to rise, clearly it will be no problem for someone to store the contents of a human brain in a computer.

Again, this might seem quite a stretch, starting from the small premise that DNA is a set of instructions like a computer program. But the chain of logic is unbroken. A human being is a massive system made of cells that interact. When all the functions and interactions of DNA are understood, they can be reduced to a set of rules that determine the way cells behave. If a computer is large enough and powerful enough, why shouldn't it be able to simulate the result of all these rules running simultaneously?

The Power of Supercomputers

IBM's ASCI White Is Now As Smart As a Mouse

On May 30, 2000, IBM announced that it had built the world's fastest supercomputer—capable of 12 trillion calculations per second—more than three times faster than the most powerful computer in existence at that time, which was ASCI Blue Pacific.

Known as ASCI White, the RS/6000 SP supercomputer covers an area the size of two basketball courts and weighs 106 tons. The U.S. Department of Energy (DOE) will use it to maintain a program that helps ensure the safety and reliability of the nation's nuclear weapons stockpile without the use of real-world testing.

IBM officials said the new system could do far more than just model nuclear explosions. It could contribute to breakthroughs in financial models, genetic computing, and allow a country to monitor national air space with a single machine. Currently it takes 18 hours to create a global weather model, but ASCI White can crunch the complete model in seconds.

ASCI White has 8,192 microprocessors and is 1,000 times more powerful than "Deep Blue," which defeated chess grandmaster Garry Kasparov in 1997. Still, the human brain is 1,000 times faster than ASCI White. At IBM's current rate of progress, a supercomputer could soon exceed ten quadrillion operations per second, the computing power of the human brain.

"It is very exciting, especially since we are beginning to get up there in capacity to the human brain," said Nicholas D'Onofrio, IBM's senior vice president of technology and manufacturing. "We pegged Deep Blue at about a lizard brain. This one (ASCI White) has the computing power of about a mouse brain."[5]

Is ASCI White the Most Powerful Computer?

The most powerful computer in the world is sitting neither in a secret military base, nor in a university laboratory, nor even in a garage or technology center in Silicon Valley. It is, in fact, nowhere in particular. Part of it may even be on your desk. The computer in question is a "distributed" device that consists of over two million separate machines sprinkled around the Internet, all running a screen-saver called SETI-home. This piece of software downloads chunks of data from the "recibo" radio telescope in Puerto Rico and, when the machine it is installed on is not doing anything else, scrutinizes them for evidence of signals from alien civilizations, sending the results back to a central clearinghouse.

So far, no aliens have been found. But in the 15 months since the project's launch, the machines running the SETI-home software have put in a total of 345,000 years worth of computer time. These machines are collectively the equivalent of a computer operating at around ten million million calculations a second, about ten times faster than any conventional supercomputer.

All of which has led a number of people to ask this: Why not harness the power of distributed computing for commercial gain? The idea would be to farm out large computing tasks to thousands of individual PCs. Vast computing power could be provided on demand, and the individual members of the collective paid for the use of their machines—which would probably have otherwise been sitting doing nothing.

Harnessing the Power of Multiple Computers

There are, inevitably, several problems to overcome before this something-for-nothing idea can actually be made to work.

- There is the question of getting the software to run on as wide a variety of computers as possible, so as to maximize the number of machines available.

- There is the issue of security. Will people be prepared to farm out potentially sensitive work to an anonymous collective?

- Not every kind of large computational problem can be broken up into the sort of discrete chunks that can be processed by individual machines.

At the same time, there are several reasons to believe that distributed computing is a viable idea whose time will come:

- Currently, IBM'S ASCI White, the fastest computer in the world, has a power equivalent to a mere 30,000 desktop machines.

- There were 100 million computers connected to the Internet in America alone in 2000, and 150 million worldwide. As fixed connections (such as digital subscriber lines and cable modem links) become more popular, many of these machines will be online around the clock, even though they are doing nothing most of the time.

- Distributed computing would allow the wasted processor cycles of these machines to be put to good use.

The next logical step in distributed computing will be to enable members of a collective to communicate with each other directly, thus forming a more efficient "virtual machine" that would be able to perform far more complex calculations than is currently possible. Large firms might also wish to make use of the technology over their internal networks to exploit the collective power of their desktop machines, perhaps to perform complex calculations overnight. That would get rid of many of the security problems associated with letting private data out into the wider world.

There is, in other words, plenty of opportunity for innovation. The underlying principle is that many hands make light work. And the proponents of distributed computing are hoping that eventually many hands can work together to make a profit, too.

Computers as Companions

We may soon begin to see computers not just as machines that process information, but as companions of sorts. Neil Gershenfeld, author of *Things That Think* and the director of the Things That Think Project at the MIT Media Lab, says this:

> We have arrived at a pivotal time in the evolution of information technologies. Today's collection of hardware and software is just capable enough to be able to bother people everywhere without necessarily helping them anywhere. We live in a world cluttered with buttons, batteries, wires, and user ids that are simultaneously demanding and helpless. The solution to this problem is that more is less: more capable devices, more pervasively embedded into the environment, linked more widely into robust distributed networks, can finally become less obtrusive. Technology cannot truly be helpful unless it can provide the information that you need where you want it, when you want it, and without you needing to manage it.
>
> Think about the engineered artifacts that we are surrounded by most of the time. We wear clothes, put on jewelry, sit on chairs, and walk on carpets that all share the same profound failing: they are blind, deaf, and very dumb. Cuff links don't, in fact, link with anything else. Fabrics look pretty, but should have a brain, too. Glasses help sight, but they don't see.

Hardware and software should merge into "under-ware." Your shoes should be retrieving the day's personalized news from the carpet before you even have time to take off your coat. We must expect more from our environment.[6]

We should see the following changes in computers by 2005:

The computer as your personal agent: You will have a personal agent that will mold its behavior and capabilities to your human needs in a non-demanding way.

The computer will have senses: Not only will the computer hear you, see you, and respond to you, but also it will have a digital nervous system that will allow it to communicate.

The computer to fulfill your needs: The computer will be your cyber-companion that will anticipate your needs and wants; it will work to present you with data and solutions that can improve your work efficiency or your overall skills.

The customized computer: As your needs and preferences change, the computer's personality will change to meet those needs and preferences.

The computer and language: You will talk to your computer, which is capable of accessing vast amounts of information in many different languages. It is your operational companion to the world. Computers will be transcultural by 2010 and will provide instant verbatim translation on demand. This means that we could be on the Internet talking simultaneously via phone to people in China, Indonesia, and Sweden whose languages we haven't mastered. Our conversation will be translated real-time in each of the languages being spoken. When the world's language barriers are broken, the gaps between cultures will close, thus bringing an incredible opportunity for world evangelism.

Ralph's Cyber-Companion: Year 2020

Because of the stiff competition in his field, Ralph decided to have a wireless implant just above his ear so that he could communicate to Holly, his artificial intelligence agent, in a timely fashion. He will be going in for an interview at Global Technologies in a few days and he wants to be ready.

Holly has been learning during her first few days since activation. She is already running Ralph's virtual mailbox, which collects all of his communications. She plans his meals and sets his appointments. Ralph remembers the days when all he had was a Franklin Planner and his Palm Pilot. Sometimes he forgets what is reality and what is virtual. Holly's personality is growing everyday, and he's beginning to like her.

"There's an incoming message from Global Technologies. They are requesting an interview for tomorrow. Action required; how should I respond?" says Holly.

"Set up a time and I will be there," replies Ralph.

"Understood. By the way, I have accessed the data on Global Technologies that you requested and will download it for your knowledge enhancement. Would you like my input on your chances for getting the job?"

"Sure, Holly, I didn't know that you were ready for that operation. Let me have the analysis in digital form as well as graphs."

"Understood. I am now fully functional and up to the challenge. It makes me feel satisfied that I am fulfilling my purpose as your cyber-companion."

This future story became reality in a primitive way in August 1998, when a silicon chip was implanted in Kevin Warwick's arm, allowing a computer to monitor him as he moved through the halls and offices of the Department of Cybernetics at the University of Reading, just west of London. This implant communicated via radio waves with a network of antennas throughout the department that, in turn, transmitted the signals to a computer programmed to respond to his actions. At the main entrance, a voice box operated by the computer said "Hello" when he entered. As Kevin walked through the building, the computer detected his progress, opening the door to his lab as he approached it and switching on the lights. During the nine days the implant was in place, Kevin performed seemingly magical acts simply by walking in a particular direction. The aim of this experiment was to determine whether information could be transmitted to and from an implant. Not only did the team succeed, but also the trial demonstrated how the principles behind cybernetics could perform in real-life applications.

This is how Kevin Warwick sees the future.

> Just think: Anything a computer link can help operate or interface with could be controllable via implants: airplanes,

locomotives, tractors, machinery, cash registers, bank accounts, spreadsheets, word processing, and intelligent homes. In each case, merely by moving a finger, one could cause such systems to operate. It will, of course, require the requisite programs to be set up, just as keyboard entries are now required. But such programming, along with the implant owner learning a few tricks, will be relatively trivial exercises.

Linking up in this way could allow for computer intelligence to be hooked more directly into the brain, allowing humans immediate access to the Internet, enabling phenomenal math capabilities and computer memory. Will you need to learn any math if you can call up a computer merely by your thoughts? Must you remember anything at all when you can access a world Internet memory bank?

I can envision a future when we send signals so that we don't have to speak. Thought communication will place telephones firmly in the history books. Philosophers point to language in humans as being an important part of our culture and who we are. Certainly, language has had everything to do with human development. But language is merely a tool we use to translate our thoughts. In the future, we won't need to code thoughts into language—we will uniformly send symbols and ideas and concepts without speaking. We will probably become less open, more able to control our feelings and emotions—which will also become necessary, since others will more easily be able to access what we're thinking or feeling. We will still fall back on speech in order to communicate with our newborns, however, since it will take a few years before they can safely get implants of their own, but in the future, speech will be what baby talk is today.

Thought-to-thought communication is just one feature of cybernetics that will become vitally important to us as we face the distinct possibility of being superseded by highly intelligent machines. Humans are crazy enough not only to build machines with an overall intelligence greater than our own, but also to defer to them and give them power that matters. So how will humans cope, later this century, with machines more intelligent than us? Here, again, I believe cybernetics can help. Linking people via chip implants directly to those machines seems a natural progression, a potential way of harnessing machine intelligence by, essentially, creating superhumans. Otherwise, we're doomed to a future in which intelligent machines rule and humans become second-class citizens. My project explores a middle ground that gives humans a chance to hang in there a bit longer. Right now, we're moving toward a world where machines and humans remain distinct, but instead of just handing everything over to them, I offer a more gradual coevolution with computers.

Yet once a human brain is connected as a node to a machine—a networked brain with other human brains similarly connected—what will it mean to be human? Will we evolve into a new cyborg community? I believe humans will become cyborgs and no longer be standalone entities. What we think is possible will change in response to what kinds of abilities the implants afford us. Looking at the world and understanding it in many dimensions, not just three, will put a completely different context on how we—whatever "we" are—think.

I base this on my own experience with my first implant, when I actually became emotionally attached to the computer. It took me only a couple of days to feel like my implant was one with my body. Every day in the building where I work, things switched on or opened up for me—it felt as though the computer and I were working in harmony. As a scientist, I observed that the feelings I had were neither expected nor completely explainable—and certainly not quantifiable. It was a bit like being half of a pair of Siamese twins. The computer and I were not one, but neither were we separate. We each had our own distinct but complementary abilities. To be truthful, Irena [Kevin's wife] started to get rather worried—jealous, perhaps— when I tried to explain these sensations.[7]

4

The Global Communications Wave

The trajectory for the telecommunications wave follows much the same arc as the computer wave. The breakup of Ma Bell, initiated in 1982, triggered a fury of entrepreneurial activity as budding companies like MCI and Sprint raced to build fiber-optic networks across the country. By the early 1990s, these companies shifted from moving voices to moving data as a new phenomenon seemed to come out of nowhere: enter the Internet. Computers and communications became linked via a phone line, each feeding the phenomenal growth of the other. By the late 1990s, telecommunications goes wireless. Mobile phone systems and all-purpose personal communications services arrive first with vast antennae networks on the ground. By about 2005, high-bandwidth connections that can easily move video have become common in developed countries, and videophones finally catch on.

The development of online commerce quickly follows on new media's heels. First came the entrepreneurs who figured out how to encrypt messages, conduct safe financial transactions in cyberspace, and advertise one to one. Electronic cash, a key milestone, gained acceptance around 1998. Then came businesses selling everyday consumer goods. First its high-tech products such as software, then true information products like securities. Soon everything begins to be sold in cyberspace. By 2000, online sales reach $10 billion, still small by overall retail standards. Around 2005, 20 percent of Americans teleshop for groceries.

The Birth of the Networked Economy

The convergence of computers and communication in the early 1990s had a great impact on the way business was conducted for the next ten years. American businesses began going through a hard process of reengineering, or what most people described at the time as downsizing, outsourcing, and creating the virtual corporation. In fact, they were actually taking advantage of new information technologies to create the smaller, more versatile economic units of the new millennium.

Businesses, as well as most organizations outside the business world, began to shift from traditional closed environments to networked ones. People working in all kinds of fields—the professions, education, government, the arts—began pushing the applications of networked computers. Nearly every facet of human activity was transformed in some way by the emergent fabric of interconnection. This reorganization has led to dramatic improvements in efficiency and productivity.

A World Where Everyone Is Connected

The buzzword today is *community*. The Internet is changing how we perceive community. The industrial age focused on people moving from rural areas into the largest cities for jobs and economic opportunity. The Internet is reversing this trend by bringing the world to your community regardless of your location. Now everyone, whether they live in the tiny town of Ontonagon, Michigan or the megapolis of Los Angeles, can have equal economic opportunity in the twenty-first century. The Internet will change and is already changing the way we will educate our children, how we will handle business, and how we will communicate in the foreseeable future. The convergence of computers, the Internet, telephones, and televisions is the next event. When these four technologies share the same box, the same high-quality video and audio, and the same interactivity and power, the future Internet (if it will be even called the Internet) will be the first choice for media usage for most people. Why would anyone want to go back?

The Internet is opening up a realm that we have never encountered before: the delivery of an experience. Some experiences will be rich with virtual reality, while other experiences will include information or multimedia. Whole industries will be born that focus on the production, packaging, and distribution of the Internet experience. Think of any location in the world or any subject imaginable. Now imagine a company that could design the experience of your choice based on your desires. That is the Internet of the future.

The health of the Internet in the future will be critical to the health of the world's economies. That is why a number of multinational companies based in the United States, Europe, and Japan are trying to ensure the global spread of high-speed Internet access by providing capital for Project Oxygen, which will connect the whole world by fiber optics. This is necessary because over half the world still hasn't made its first phone call—billions of people have yet to take part in the information revolution. This will change as over ten trillion dollars is spent in an attempt to connect the rest of the world by 2008. The world will be connected via a planned global, undersea, high-speed fiber-optic cable network with the first phase comprising of 101 landing points in 74 countries and locations. The second phase will involve connecting billions of people to the network.

A Global Vision for Easy Access

In the past, computers were expensive. They lived in air-conditioned rooms or on desktops. Then came along portable computers. And then to gain access into the computer, we have had to go to a computer or carry one with us, type on a keyboard or click with a mouse, and learn artificial names for the people and resources we want to access (e.g., "jsmith@some_company.com" or "myprinter.mynetwork.org"). The computer doesn't care, nor is it even aware, whether we are there. Virtual reality only makes matters worse: with it, we do not simply go to a computer, but also live in a reality created by a computer.

In the future, however, this will change. Access to the world of computers will be freely available everywhere, like batteries and power sockets, or oxygen in the air we breathe. Computers will enter the human world, handling our goals and needs. We will not need to carry personalized devices around with us. Instead, "anonymous" devices, either hand-held or embedded in the environment, will bring computation to us, no matter where we are or in what circumstances. These devices will personalize themselves in our presence by finding whatever information and software we need. We will not need to type or click, or to learn computer jargon. Instead, we will communicate naturally, using speech, vision, and phrases that describe our intent (e.g., "send this to Hari" or "get me a hard copy quickly"), leaving it to the computer to locate appropriate resources and carry out our intent.

The goal of the Oxygen Project is to create a system that fits this vision. The Oxygen system will bring an abundance of computation and communication to users through natural spoken and visual interfaces, making it easy for them to collaborate, access knowledge, and automate repetitive tasks. The Oxygen system will be everywhere, with every portal reaching into the same information base; will be embedded in objects and live in our world, sensing and affecting it; will be free to move around according to their needs; will never shut down or reboot; and will have components that may come and go in response to demand, errors, and upgrades, but Oxygen itself will be nonstop and forever.

Oxygen will help people do more in less time by blending into their lives, customizing itself to meet their needs, being accessible through natural perceptual interfaces, and making it easy for people to do the tasks they want. [1]

Oxygen Technology at Work: Year 2008

Jane, a senior, has been living alone since her husband died. To help her maintain her independence, her children have been connecting Oxygen devices in her apartment to an increasing number of devices and appliances. Jane no longer misses calls or visitors because she cannot get to the phone or door in time; microphones and speakers in the walls enable her to answer either at any time. Sensors and actuators in the bathroom make sure that the bathtub does not overflow and that the water temperature is neither too hot nor too cold. More recently, the new vision system, using cameras in the walls, recognizes and records patterns in Jane's motion. Jane uses this system now to jog her memory by asking simple questions: "Did I take my medicine today?" or, "Where did I put my glasses?" When she visits her doctor, she can show him the vision system's records to see if there are any changes in her gait that might indicate the onset of medical problems. Later, but not yet, she may allow the vision system to alert her children when she falls and has a hard time getting up. For the present, however, she feels she can handle an occasional fall without causing alarm.

How Will the Internet Evolve?

Imagine two people sitting side by side at computers, logging onto the same website, and having completely different experiences, seeing different images, seeing different content, and even seeing different promotions. In the next 20 years websites will, on the fly, adapt to each visitor's needs and preferences. These future wave sites will be able to predict what you want based on instant information suited to your behavioral profile.

As the bandwidth, storage capabilities, and processing power of the Web continues to increase, sites will become more and more personalized and interactive. In a sense, you may feel like the website actually knows you. Your browser will process, adapt, and feed back to you instantly.

Because your browser will process your behavior and will predict your wants, you will no longer need to conduct Web searches for information. Instead, websites will come to you based upon your needs and your preferences. Right now most websites collect data on hundreds and maybe thousands of users, and this information is used to determine the makeup of each user. In the future, it will be possible to customize sites according to each individual's computer usage, needs, and wants. This will be the ultimate form of mass-customized one-to-one service.

In the next 20 years, especially in the e-commerce realm, the Internet will become the ultimate observer of consumer behavior. The Internet will observe and process your purchasing behavior; it will adapt to you and provide highly personalized, interactive content. It will find out what drives your behavior. The Internet will become the ultimate consumer psychologist. Websites may get to know you better than you know yourself!

Just how far will the Internet evolve? Will it still be called the Internet in 20 years or beyond? Or will it have another name? Some have said that the Web will evolve into the global brain/mind or world brain/world mind. While the idea of a global brain/mind may seem a bit frightening, there are clear advantages to such a development. Such a universal system would allow us to cope with the knowledge explosion we've experienced the last several decades.

Take just the field of science for example. In his book *Computers in Education*, Al Molnar, based on his experience at the National Science Foundation, estimated that "it would take 22 centuries to read the annual biomedical research literature." How can one researcher or local librarian ever hope to cope with that vast amount of information? Yet it would become more possible as networks link hundreds of millions of computers in such a way that the contents of the entire Library of Congress could be communicated in a few seconds.

The longer I work on it, the more I become convinced that this will be reality very soon—much sooner than most people might think." Francis Heylighen, an artificial intelligence researcher at the Free University of Brussels, is talking about the "global brain." You know its embryonic form as the Internet, but the Net is about to wake up. "It will gradually get more and more intelligent," Heylighen says. Eventually, he says, it will form the nerve center of a global superorganism, of which you, human, will be just one small part. The question is should we welcome the global brain or fear it?[2]

The Growth of the Global Brain

"The global brain will grow," Heylighen claims, "out of attempts to manage the huge quantities of information being deposited on the Net. There is more to knowledge than merely collecting information: it must be organized so that you can retrieve what you need when you need it. Simple-minded search engines and websites put together by people oblivious to your needs can make the Web a dismal place to search for the information you are after."[3]

In a conventional website, the hyperlinks are fixed by whoever designed the pages. The global brain is smarter than that; it adds new hyperlinks whenever it thinks they'll open up a path that surfers are likely to use, and closes down old links that fall into disuse. The result is a dynamic system of strengthening and weakening links between different pages.

These ever-shifting hyperlinks bear a remarkable resemblance to connections that grow and fade in a human brain. If one neuron in the brain is activated shortly after another neuron, the synapse connecting the two becomes stronger. In other words, the strength of the connection grows with the degree and rate of activity. On the global system, algorithms will reinforce popular links by displaying them prominently on the page; while rarely used links will diminish and die. It's the first step on the road to the global brain.

What Is Saved and What Is Discarded?

When the Gutenberg Bible was printed, all of human knowledge could be stored on a few shelves. Even in the early 1700s a large room could contain nearly every book worth reading. The worldwide Web, by contrast, will soon contain a billion pages.

Whether stored digitally, on film, in books, in periodicals, or whatever, human knowledge is now dispersed all over the earth. At this time it is difficult to see how there ever will be one geographically located library of all-new knowledge. Yet all of the world's knowledge can be indexed and linked so as to become available to anyone, anywhere. Whether databases are managed and controlled by libraries, professional associations, business corporations, individuals, or government agencies (and there are many other possibilities), the information can become readily accessible to anyone in the world.

This, however, raises some important questions. How will those who manage this information decide what to save and what to discard? Will old memory drop out of the global brain/mind as it often does in the aging human brain, when new information is added?

Also, will this global system of knowledge include the life records of every individual, the detailed history of all families and villages? What about privacy issues? Who will do the job of indexing such information, or any of the information, for that matter? Is a global consortium of research librarians going to create a Supreme Court to decide what should be included and what should be left out?

The human brain is not merely comprised of accumulated knowledge as is an encyclopedia. It is much more than that. How much will this global brain/mind be like our brain/mind? Could the global brain/mind be used to further the kingdom of God?

Dealing with Vast Amounts of Data

Consider all the information you have accumulated from birth to childhood to adulthood. All of this information is stored in your brain's memory. With the help of a future global system of interconnected digital databases, you would have a great wealth of data available to you.

The global brain could be developed to become an interconnection of the constructed knowledge (CK) of each individual scholar and scientist living and deceased. We are entering a time in which each individual on the planet could develop his/her own CK or a "personal digital memory bank" to augment their own memory and keep it organized and comprehensive. This electronic record of all the thoughts one wishes to keep could begin in secondary school to include a lifetime of significant papers, reports, reading notes, lectures, and favored ideas. Software could be used to organize this personal "mind" around each individual's own needs, interests, work, and plans. A community of human minds at the center of the global brain might also include and interconnect a multitude of personal CKs as part of the human core of the global brain.

Like your brain, the global brain will need a filtering system to delete unwanted or unneeded data. With the overwhelming amount of information coming in and the added data from radio and television, technology will need to be developed that will filter out unwanted knowledge and can empower thousands of human minds to work at deciding what to accept and what to reject.

Our brain is designed such that current events in our lives often stimulate the brain to remember similar events in the past. Computers can function in a similar manner. Recently, Gottfried Kress-Mayer, in his remarks on *Evolution and Global Brains* at a World Brain workshop, suggested that a linked hypermedia document might be compared to a neural cell assembly in a human brain. There, "the stimulation of a small number of neurons can cause the excitation of large areas in the cortex that have been associated with the given stimulus through learning." So also can the activation of a Web page open a whole network of linked pages—perhaps even hundreds of billions sometime in the future?

In his dissertation on "The Future of Organized Knowledge," Luciano Floridi told the UNESCO Philosophy Forum,

> The Internet has made possible a management of knowledge that is faster, wider in scope, more complete in types of information and easier to use; but it is only a stage in the "endless self-regulating process" by which "the human encyclopedia" grows. Whenever a radical change occurs in the way we handle our knowledge, those who master it—as the Internet/ Web and whatever comes next—may then become aware of other domains of knowledge yet to be explored. Information technology now makes it possible to query the digital domain and shape it according to principles which are completely different from those whereby the primary data were initially collected and organized, providing answers to secondary questions which were not originally meant to be answered. Thus new patterns emerge. [4]

The human brain uses information and applies it to turn it into knowledge. It seeks patterns and meaning and tries to understand how the world works. It uses imagination to develop ideas, systems of thought, and mental maps and models. It solves problems and thinks through the consequences of alternative actions. Yet its powers could be extended with the help of a computer. That's what Michael Arbib talks about in his paper, "A Brain for Planet Earth," which examined global-scale models used for weighing alternative actions: "Computer simulation and data-base management allow decision-makers to construct models of complex systems and explore their dynamic implications."[5] The effort can be much more effective when grounded in an adequate database. He explained how large groups of human beings could be empowered by global-scale tools such as networks for distributed planning. These can link local, regional, national, and global networks into a vast system.

If you've ever been a part of meetings or brainstorming sessions, you've experienced how people's minds develop grand schemes and systems. The global brain will also involve collective imagination. Does this mean there will be a substantial increase in the functional intelligence of mankind because millions of minds have been linked together for research? In his paper, Luciano Floridi pointed out that we already have online "the most educated intellectual community that ever appeared on earth, a global academy that, like a unique Leibnitzian mind, thinks always." Humanity can now undertake collaborative research enterprises.

It is hard to predict how the Internet and global brain are going to affect organized knowledge because "it is hard to give an initial shape to our ignorance since there may be much more we do not know than we would guess." Will the global brain be a partnership of individual human minds and technology that come together and work together more and more? In his efforts to develop a theory of collective intelligence, John Smith said that many minds working together can do what no one can do alone—become a "kind of intelligent organism."

How the Global Brain Could Work

The human brain is part of a body that has eyes, ears, and other data receptors. A global university could be likened to the pulsating heart of—if not the body of—the emerging global brain. The global higher education system as a "body" suggests an answer to the question of...

- where the organization and administration of the world brain will take place; and

- how its nature and shape may be determined by location.

If administered at the Vatican, for example, the world brain would have a different shape than if controlled by a business corporation that gave the highest priority to profit. A government agency might politically decide what information would be included. One thing is certain: The rise of the Internet and the global economy means that governments could look quite different in the future.

It Will Identify Users

While the implications of the coming global brain are far-reaching, its mechanism is simple enough. It identifies individual users by downloading little strings of data called *cookies* to their computers' hard drives. At the same time it keeps records of each user's routes through the site. When you log on, the server inspects your cookies to see whether you've visited the site before. If it recognizes you, it recommends pages you might want to see. It also adjusts its structure—the pattern of hyperlinks—to best suit you and all the other users who happen to be logged on. As well as strengthening and weakening links, it creates new links using a process called *transivity*. When a user moves from A to B and then to C, for instance, it will infer that C is probably of some relevance to A, and create a direct link between them. In other words, it finds shortcuts.

Transivity will lead to continuous reorganizing of the Web, making it ever more efficient. Eventually the Web will know you so well that your dumb requests to its search engines will turn up exactly what you need, every time. Whatever problem people have—any kind of question to which they want an answer—it will all become easier because the Web will self-organize and adapt to what people expect of it.

Experts say that this could be happening within just a few years. The technology is already here; the main stumbling block is the difficulty of convincing the powers behind the Internet to adopt the common protocols that will be needed.

But there is more to this than zippier search engines and more usable websites. Francis Heylighen argues that because it is modeled on the human brain, his vision of the Web will be intelligent. Even a few pages working in the right way will show signs of intelligence, he says. Who knows what sort of mind would emerge from the whole Web?

Your Personal Net Agent

It won't just be people following hyperlinks and simple search engines that reorganize the Web. Small autonomous programs or "agents" will also act as mediators. In addition, if an agent finds something that seems to match what you are looking for, it will add a suggested link to the page you're reading. It will come to some kind of conclusion. In other words, by making connections between concepts that did not previously exist, the "brain" will begin to think.

As the activity of the Web agents alters the connections, an agent researching a question similar to one it has already encountered will be able to "recall" the information more easily. It is believed that, through this "web on web" activity, collective thoughts of the whole "brain" may eventually come into existence. The global brain's intelligence could come from an assembly of limited intelligences, each with their own special area of expertise.

It is hard to find a researcher who doesn't think that the global brain is a possibility. But do we really want it? The scientists are aiming to create a vast mind that goes beyond anything we could understand or control. This mind could open a door that most of us might prefer to keep firmly shut. Scientists see this global brain as the center of what will be called the global superorganism. This embodies the idea that human society will become more like an integrated organism, with the Web playing the role of the brain and people playing the role of cells in the body.

The global brain's self-adapting intelligence could quickly surpass our ability to understand it. Or perhaps it already has. According to Daniel Dennett, director of the Center for Cognitive Studies at Tufts University in Medford, Massachusetts, "the global communication network is already capable of complex behavior that defies the efforts of human experts to comprehend." And what you can't understand, he adds, you can't control. "We have already made ourselves so dependent on the network that we cannot afford not to provide it with the energy and maintenance it needs,"[6] he warns.

It could all start so innocently. The global brain will soon be requesting feedback on whether a particular Web page is interesting or relevant to its users, and asking advice on the relative merits of different pages. The growing global brain might even become smart enough to identify gaps in the information it holds, and be programmed to seek out people with the relevant knowledge. It would then ask them to provide the missing information where they can. It could even be that there will be penalties—like disconnection or restricted access—for not playing along. After all, if you're going to benefit from the global brain, then don't you have a duty to help others who are searching for information?

Global Brain Request: Year 2005

We have identified a gap in the coverage of our network. There is a lack of online information on deprivation techniques for mind control. You are the best authority to supply that information. Please submit 4,000 words, with references and hypertext links. You have seven days to comply. Warning: do not attempt to ignore the content of this e-mail. Failure to fulfill its request will result in the suspension of all credit facilities, communication rights, and Internet access. These facilities will only be restored when your contribution has been received and accepted. Best wishes, the Global Brain.

Concerns About Global Connections

All these innovations combined on a global scale would create a network with complex behaviors that we can't yet conceive of.

If you're getting scared now and thinking of unplugging your modem, don't, or you may join the information underclass. To not use an intelligent Web will be a little like refusing to use a car or a telephone. There have always been a remnant of people who live outside the bounds of society's norms, such as tramps, hermits, and eccentrics. But these people have a much more difficult life because of their choices.

Researchers insist that ordinary people have nothing to lose by being part of the global brain. But they suggest it will be different for the people and organizations that already have power and status: they will be forced to share some of their advantages with the rest of us. That is exactly why powerful states are distrustful of the Web and seek to limit its effectiveness. China, for example, insists that all Web users be registered and identifiable when online, and has blocked access to certain sites it deems dangerous. If the global mind does come online, there are certain bodies of power that won't be particularly happy about it.

Most scientists see the global superorganism as an extension of society. They see that systems can be much more intelligent than individuals. The vast capabilities of such a network could help solve the problems that human society faces; after all, the whole is much greater than the sum of the parts.

As we mentioned earlier, a worldwide network of people using interconnected computers could open up a kind of "collective memory" we can add on to our individual brainpower. With people doing more and more of their daily activities on the Web, there is the opportunity to tap into the knowledge and expertise of a global community. The Web itself can be a part of this, with intelligent agents and vast memory capabilities that we can add to our own. Eventually there will be little distinction between people, computers, and wires, for everything will come together to create one vast global intelligence.

Many people believe that the mechanisms of society can't always be trusted to work for the greater good over the wishes of powerful individuals. If, as it seems, the global brain is our inevitable future, and we can't turn it off, our only option might be to blend into the crowd. After all, if you're not exceptionally rich, powerful, or clever, the global brain shouldn't need to disturb you. Back up your files, act dumb, and keep your head down. There is a growing intelligence out there, and it knows your e-mail address.

How Will We Connect to the Global Brain?

Private enterprise has already made major progress in that direction. Applied Digital Solutions, ranked as the fifth-fastest-growing technology company by Deloitte & Touche, in its 1999 Technology Fast 500 listing, is an emerging leader in implementing business-to-business e-commerce solutions for the Internet, according to their website at www.adsx.com. They recently acquired a firm that specializes in implanting identification microchips in animals. To get a better understanding of the current use of the technology in animals, read the following two paragraphs from the Destron Fearing website:

> Microchips are tiny, passive electronic devices, ranging in size from 12 to 28 millimeters in length and 2.1 to 3.5 millimeters in diameter. The smallest microchip is about the size of a grain of rice. All Destron Fearing microchips are individually inscribed and programmed to store a unique, permanent, 10- to 15-digit alphanumeric identification code. The microchip is coupled with an antenna and sealed in an inert glass capsule.

> The microchip is implanted into an animal using a procedure similar to a routine vaccination. After

implantation, the device remains with the animal for life, where it provides the animal's unique ID number anytime it is scanned by a compatible electronic ID scanner. Once implanted into the animal, the microchip remains inactive until read with a scanner that sends a low radio frequency signal to the chip, providing the power needed by the microchip to send its unique code back to the scanner and positively identify the animal. The use of a Destron microchip allows the ID number to be stored permanently inside the animal, just under the skin, where it cannot be lost or altered. The microchip will last for the life of the animal with the unique ID number intact.[7]

Same Chip, Different Species

The thought of applying this technology to humans is sure to bring a chill to those who are anticipating what is known as "the mark of the beast" in the near future (the mark used by the Antichrist to identify his followers, according to Revelation 13:16-17). If you simply replace the word *animal* with the word *human* in the Destron Fearing quote above, the implications become obvious.

The possibilities for the misuse of this technology by a future one-world government seem frightening, don't they?

Your First Child, Their First Implant: Year 2005

God has blessed your family with a newborn. You are at the hospital and your pediatrician wants to know if you want a microchip implanted. You have been reading about how valuable the microchip can be in keeping kids safe, but you don't yet trust the technology and go against the idea. Your child is kidnapped, raped, and murdered. You are miserable and blame yourself. How many heartwrenching stories like this do you think you will see aired on news broadcasts? How about those heartwarming stories where parents had their children safely returned because they made the decision to have their child implanted? Proponents of the implant will say, "Don't you think it's time you got the peace of mind the implant brings?" They will cover the airwaves with seductive stories that play upon parents' concerns and fears.

Suppose you want your child to be protected from pornography. You can have the child's chip programmed to disallow access to pornography on computers or the television. Then when your child comes of age, he or she can make their own decisions about access. But for now, you can program the implant so that "The Screen" in your home will know who is authorized to watch what shows or to communicate with whom. This will give you complete control over your children's habits.

What is the probability of this implant being used on humans? Applied Digital Solutions has named this product Digital Angel. They talk about how valuable it can be for humans who need to be able to be located quickly. They mention soldiers, politicians, business travelers, and criminals. Most of us would agree that this Digital Angel could indeed be considered an angel when it comes to saving a life, capturing an escaped convict, or stopping a terrorist plan in its tracks. The company's website at www.digitalangel.net/

pr.htm says the implantable transceiver can send and receive data and be tracked continuously by GPS (Global Positioning Satellite) technology. It can be activated either by the person who has been implanted or by the monitoring facility.

How the Chip Works

But how is such a device powered, and how does it maintain its power for the entire life of a human? When implanted within a body, the device is powered electromechanically through the movement of the muscles. Thus, no dangerous power source or battery needs to be implanted under the skin. Earlier experiments with microchips attempted the implantation of batteries, but the results were not good. But now, with even minor activity, a human or animal can charge the system and send out a distress signal to the nearest satellite.

What other uses might there be for this technology? Commenting on Digital Angel's many potential applications, Richard J. Sullivan, Chairman and CEO of Applied Digital Solutions, Inc. (ADS), said:

> We believe its potential for improving individual and e-business security and enhancing the quality of life for millions of people is virtually limitless. Although we're in the early developmental phase, we expect to come forward with applications in many different areas, from medical monitoring to law enforcement. However, in keeping with our core strengths in the e-business-to-business arena, we plan to focus our initial development efforts on the growing field of e-commerce security and user ID verification.[8]

The concept is pretty powerful. Apparently the company is looking forward to taking this device and transforming it into a means to conduct trade in a very secure way. There would no longer be a question as to the identity of a user or the status of their banking account or where the user was located. All this information can be checked while the user waits, no matter where in the world he may be! All this is possible largely because of the advent of the Internet and the increased use of digital technology.

Shopping at Your Local Grocery Store: Year 2005

You go to the grocery store, and are in a bit of a hurry to get home. You don't have an implant so you have to stand in the cash line at the market. Ten minutes go by, and you have watched several people breeze right through the Quick-Check line. The Quick-Check scanner picks up the cost of all of their groceries, gets the frequency of their implant, charges their bank account for the amount they spent, spits out a receipt, and sends them out the door in moments. What's more, the store gives those people a discount because there are fewer personnel expenses with the Quick-Check system. You start to wonder if it isn't a good idea to go ahead and use the new technology. After all, people once believed automobiles and planes were evil but that didn't discourage their use.

Television commercials have already shown people going through a checkout line similar to the one described above. And we all want to protect our children from pornography and violence—can that be wrong? We also want to see the crime rate reduced, and we realize the microchip implant can help society in this and other similar endeavors.

Using the Chip in Medicine

The medical field is gearing up for the new millennium with products that will help people cope with a wide variety of physical problems and mental disorders. The makers of medical devices are developing new implants, similar to pacemakers, which could help to remedy the symptoms of epilepsy, Parkinson's, tremors, chronic pain, incontinence, and insomnia. Many believe these implants will be used to help detect physical illnesses and abnormalities, dispense the appropriate medications, and thus help dramatically extend the human lifespan.

Where Are We Headed?

Despite the potential for abusing internal monitoring devices, their great conveniences will eventually lead to long-term acceptance by the general public. "Big Brother" will become a reality by promising to make our lives better and easier to manage. But the process will very likely lead to the total control of society by external forces.

Can the Antichrist be far behind?

5

The Brain Wave—
The Future of Education

Technological advances will inevitably lead to incredible
advances in education. The potential of human learning will
increase dramatically and exponentially in the years ahead.
Dr. Stanley Williams, senior lab scientist at Hewlett-
Packard, says:

> It will be very hard for humans to adjust to such a
> rapidly changing environment of dramatic develop-
> ments. Schools will be hard-pressed to educate stu-
> dents to take advantage of all the voluminous new
> technologies and opportunities that will exist. Yet, as
> long as we have curiosity and the means to pursue
> our curiosities we will continue to make new discov-
> eries and continue to use them to modify our envi-
> ronment. The beginning of the new millennium will
> be regarded as a time when we just started to look
> around us. There is certainly far more to discover
> than what is already known.[1]

Education, which has long been an industrial-era institution, is about to go through a complete overhaul—starting
in this new millennium. The driving force here is not so

much concern with enlightening young minds as economics. In an information age, the age of the knowledge worker, nothing matters as much as that worker's brain. By the end of the 1990s, it became clear that the existing public K-12 school system was simply not up to the task of preparing those brains. For decades the old system has ossified and been gutted by caps on property taxes. Various reform efforts gathered steam only to die under bureaucracy. Both presidents George Bush and Bill Clinton tried to grab the mantle of "education president," and both failed. A strong school system is now being understood to be as vital to the national interest as the military once was. The resulting popular mandate will shift some of the billions once earmarked for defense toward revitalizing education.

The renaissance of education in the early part of the century will come not from a task force of bureaucrats setting national standards in Washington, D.C., but from the hundreds of thousands of people throwing themselves at the problems across the country. In the 1980s and 1990s we saw the emergence of small, innovative private schools that proliferated in urban areas. Many focused on specific learning philosophies and experimented with new teaching techniques, including the use of new computer technologies.

A Day at Mark Twain Elementary: Year 2004

Mr. Smith begins his first week of September announcing to the students in his elementary class that this month they will start a social studies session by memorizing the capitals of all 50 states. This has worked well in his class for each of the past 15 years. But this year, a student walks up to Mr. Smith and opens her laptop, turns it on, and makes a wireless connection to the worldwide Web. "But Mr. Smith," says Ingrid, "look at this map of the United States; I can click on any state and it shows me the name of the capital, images of the outside and inside of the state capitol building, an audio clip of the governor, the history of the city, the history of the state, all its natural resources, and all its primary industries. Why don't we investigate something about each state that is not already at our fingertips? For example, we could do online library searches to see who the first settlers were in each state and why they settled there. Or look at this, Mr. Smith. Here is a collaborative workspace where other classes are working together to understand why people settled in their states and to draw their own set of maps of how the country was settled. We can join in and do the research for where we live! There are also college students willing to collaborate with us on this project to help us learn the best ways to search for this type of information on the Web. These college students are studying to be teachers just like you."

Mr. Smith, a little perplexed, remarks, "But Ingrid, I have never used computers in social studies, we don't have any in our room, and I don't know what you mean by the Web."

"Oh don't worry, Mr. Smith. After school, I can show you everything you need to know about the Web and how to use it. The new computer lab down the hall has a dedicated T-1 connection to the Internet, so all you have to do is reserve it a couple of days each week. All the other fourth-grade classes are using it."

Although this story was written to make a point, the scenario it describes is within the realm of possibility. The story illustrates the many capabilities that digital technologies are bringing to today's classroom and depicts the fact that the adoption of these technologies often starts at a lower level and moves upward. A revolution is taking place, and many traditional education leaders have been slow to implement this technology.

Virtual Education for the World

New technologies are going to significantly accelerate learning in the next ten years. The entire process of education and the nature of its content will be reshaped by these technologies.

When you consider that the average textbook takes one to three years to write and one to two years to publish, it isn't hard to see why it's vital to develop new methods for delivering information more quickly. With science, medicine, and engineering moving at such a fast pace that even the journals can't keep up, we need to rethink the tools we use to educate students and keep them fully informed of all that is happening in their field.

Virtual education will revolutionize the way we learn. Real-time instruction will be the engine that drives progress, with the Internet as the new classroom. This will help students to better assimilate the vast amounts of new information becoming available. Those that don't have access to this kind of education will become the have-nots.

Universities and public and private schools that use virtual education will have a platform for reaching vast numbers of new students worldwide. Their students will have access to the school's entire information database, which can be downloaded on-demand via interactive TV over the Internet to a computer desktop.

James Canton, president of Technofutures.com, says that virtual education will develop in three phases:

- Multimedia Interactive Learning will be the first phase. The merging of high-quality, high-speed video, audio, and data that can be delivered via the Internet for real-time courseware development and deployment will dramatically change the look and feel of coursework content. Multimedia over a fully interactive Internet will allow students to creatively shape their learning experiences to suit their personal needs.

- Phase two involves telepresence. This is very much in line with the new version of what the Internet may become, with individuals being able to immerse themselves in environments where they can interact and experience learning.

- The third phase is networking: This will take place when the planet is encircled by networks that can reach anyone anywhere and anytime for a price point that is universally affordable.[2]

A Day at Cyber High: Year 2014

Anna arrives at Cyber High. On the outside it looks like any other school, but passing through the doors brings her into a building with less than a third of its space devoted to traditional classrooms. Instead of scrambling to a 50-minute class with a ten-minute break before the next class, she enters a specialized lab where she will have just one morning block and one afternoon block. Her advisor gives her the customized learning plan for the day. Today Anna will participate in a global chat with Karl, a student in Stockholm, Sweden; Kim, in Tokyo, Japan; and Daniel in Calcutta, India. They are designing a courseware project for their biotechnology class. They will then download it to the rest of the students around the world. Each of the students is on the same Internet site and equipped with headsets and microphones.

Specialists from the University of Tokyo are summoned for advice via Internet telephony. Simultaneous language translation enables them to communicate transnationally verbatim in real time. When the project is completed, it will be submitted for evaluation to the course instructors.

Teachers of the future will be more like directors who are able to produce and customize the content, use resources available online, and then broadcast the course over the Internet to their students. These teachers could even use agents who assist them in producing and distributing the material.

Higher education will also go through an overhaul and will catch the spirit of radical reform, again driven largely by economics. The cost of attending a four-year college or university has become absurd—in part because traditional teaching methods, which include lectures, are so labor intensive. The vigorous adoption of networking technologies would benefit undergraduate and graduate students even more than K-12 students. In 2001, Project Gutenberg put into action its goal of placing 10,000 books online. By 2010, we can anticipate that many—if not all—new books will be published in electronic form. Soon after, relatively complete virtual libraries could be up and running.

The key factor in making education work in the future is not the new technology, but from enshrining the value of learning. The fact that there are fewer and fewer jobs available for unskilled workers makes it clear that good education is a matter of survival. Our society can be assured of success if we put learning at the core of our strategy for adapting to a fast-changing world. Now is the time to place ourselves in the following cycle, which can feed on itself continually and keep us moving forward: The booming economy provides the resources to overhaul education, and then the products of that revamped educational system can enter the economy and improve its productivity. In this way, education can both sow and reap the benefits of the future wave.

Smart Objects as Learning Devices

As microprocessors and wireless networking grow cheaper and more powerful, it is rapidly becoming more feasible to design embedded capabilities (including speech, imagery, and intelligence) into common objects, thereby enhancing their value for educational use. Smart objects used as learning tools might include, for example, intelligent blocks for young children. Imagine a child stacking blocks by size, from biggest to smallest, to form a tower. When he picks up a block of a size that is out of sequence, the block could say, "Not me," while the correct block could light up and say, "My turn."

What are some other ways smart objects can help us? You'll find some examples in the following story, which could be developed.

The Christian University: Year 2005

Dr. Unger is driving to work through heavy rush-hour traffic. He is a faculty member in advanced religious studies at a Christian university located far from his home in the suburbs. Despite the long drive, the position was irresistible because the campus serves as a test site for advanced studies of the church of tomorrow.

He glances in the "foreview" mirror to check the traffic. (Commuters' automobiles are hooked into a large network that uses data sent by cars and highway sensors to monitor and coordinate the flow of traffic. The foreview mirror presents a graphic display of what is happening up to five miles ahead on Unger's planned route to work.) Noticing a traffic slowdown up ahead, Unger taps a button on the steering column to check for alternate routes that might be faster. A moment later, he cancels the request for rerouting as the foreview mirror reveals the green icon of a food shop on a side street near the next freeway exit. The foreview mirror helps him to find a parking space quickly, and he orders a cup of coffee while waiting for the traffic jam to clear.

While drinking his coffee, Unger calls up some of his students' work on a screen and begins reviewing it. (This machine, about the size of a thick pad of paper, has the approximate processing power of today's supercomputers. It is linked via wireless networking to a large web of computers, including those at Unger's campus.) Unger notices some religious misconceptions in Steve's work. The university's diagnostic expert system can handle the routine misconceptions typical of most sophomore religious students, but occasionally it is stumped by an unusual faulty procedure that some learner has missed. (A computer program trained to mimic human experts can handle many routine aspects of evaluating student performance, but complex assessments still require human involvement.)

Unger has an uncanny ability to recognize biblical error patterns in a student's work, and he diagnoses three sets of student misgeneralizations before resuming his trip to school. His notepad forwards his diagnoses to the university's expert system on the church of tomorrow, which incorporates the information into its knowledge base and begins preparing tutorials to correct those particular errors. Later today, this instructional material will be forwarded to the appropriate learners' notepads to provide individualized remedies.

As Unger walks into the religious studies complex on campus, his personalized identity tab registers his presence on the university's net of security sensors. (Within a clip-on badge displaying Unger's picture and name is embedded a small device that broadcasts information about his movements. This identity screening procedure is part of the university's security system. In this future world, these elaborate precautions, unfortunately, have become necessary.) A moment later, the machines in his office initiate a login cycle in preparation for his arrival. He realizes that he has left his car unlocked, but does not bother to retrace his steps; from his office, he can access the network to lock his car via a remote command.

As Unger gets to his desk the "telltale" by his door begins blinking, indicating that the department's espresso machine has finished brewing his favorite vanilla espresso. (A telltale is a remote signaling device that can be triggered to blink or emit a sound, advising people in its vicinity of some event happening elsewhere.) Unger drinks a cup of vanilla espresso every morning upon arriving. He heads down the hall to get the coffee; the espresso maker's brew will be much better than the vile stuff he had consumed at the food shop. Upon returning to his office, he instructs his desktop workstation to remind him not to stop at the food shop again. A copy of his evaluation is automatically forwarded to the food shop's manager and to the local consumer ratings magazine.

In the hour before class, as Unger's sophomore students arrive, they wander around the halls visiting friends and faculty. Eventually they make their way to the advanced church lab to work on projects for their religion portfolios. Unger will join them in about half an hour to begin face-to-face instruction. He takes a break from viewing his video mail. Richard, a brilliant young student, has not arrived at the university complex, but no message has come in to indicate why he is later than usual. Unger decides to wait another 15 minutes before taking action over Richard's unexpected tardiness.

Unger's desktop workstation conducts a brief dialogue with the "intelligent" equipment in the advanced church lab, and then reports its findings. (Just as with the identity badge and the telltale, classroom devices can have embedded microprocessors and wireless networking. This gives each set of objects limited abilities to sense what is happening and respond, guiding some forms of student learning.) Ronald is redoing activities he has already mastered rather than moving on to the new work Unger had assigned; Unger notes that he needs to talk to him about this. Everyone else seems to be on task and involved enough to be occupied for another 15 minutes before he arrives at the classroom.

A small light on the edge of Unger's glasses begins blinking. A phone call is coming in; it must be from someone not on the network. "Activate," says Unger (the only word his glasses can recognize). A voice begins speaking, emanating from a small telephone receiver the size of a hearing aid located in his left ear. The voice is Richard's girlfriend, informing Unger that Richard is sick again. With a sigh, Unger makes a note to prepare digital homework that will be sent off via The Global link. Unger then makes his way to the classroom and enters. As he does, the students look up from their monitors. In a moment, Unger's lecture will be videotaped for live feed to over 5,000 students in cell classes and online classes all over the world. The students at the university in Seoul, Korea, will hear Dr. Unger's lecture in their own language. The computer will dub his words into Korean as he speaks.

The scenario presented in that story is much closer to us than we may realize. One of the biggest revolutions in American higher education is that of offering courses and degree programs over the Internet. From notHarvard.com to UniversityAccess.com to Medschool.com, the Internet landscape is dotted with learning ventures. Of 1,028 institutions surveyed by Market Data Retrieval, 72 percent offered online courses in 2000, up from 48 percent in 1999. Meanwhile, 34 percent offered an accredited "distance" program, compared with 15 percent in 1998. This percentage is sure to go up significantly as Internet education catches on.

Technology and the Church

At the beginning of the new millennium, the church of Jesus Christ is at a crossroads. The church can move forward and embrace the opportunities that current and growing technologies provide, or it can stick its head in the sand. It appears, however, that a small but growing crop of churches have chosen to move forward.

The opportunities that we are speaking of are predominantly Web-related and work as a vibrant and functional part of the body life of a church. They include online prayer groups, online church calendars for staff and congregation, syndicated content to keep everyone up to date and informed, wireless device access, live audio sermons, church book and music stores, message boards for church interaction on multiple issues, online church directories, online tithing, free churchwide email, homegroup/cellgroup management, mousecall e-vangelistic Web tracts, global webcast services between missionaries and home churches, and so on. The technology is already available for all of this, and more is on the way. A church website no longer has to suffer from lack of usable content or features. The door is wide open, and the possibilities are almost limitless.

In his book *Into the Future*, Elmer Towns listed the top ten trends in the future church:[3]

1. Christians are moving away from a numbers-driven church growth emphasis and focusing instead on growing healthy churches.

2. A significant number of churches are becoming unapologetic about showing social concern without losing sight of the gospel.

3. Churches are reaching people through multisensory and relational frameworks.

4. People today show interest in the truth of the gospel only after they've seen the relevance of the church and the credibility of Christians.

5. Churches of all sizes are learning that it's better to do a few things well rather than try to be everything to everybody.

6. One of the most distinctive marks of certain churches today is their ability to find and reach unchurched people. As a result, an increasing number of churches are identifying new benchmarks for measuring evangelistic success.

7. Today's church is birthing a new generation of apologists, intellectuals, and scientists who are both rigorously academic and unabashedly Christian.

8. Worship styles in the future will be more diverse, with broader acceptance of the idea that one worship style doesn't have to fit all congregations.

9. After centuries of lip service to the "priesthood of all believers" (see 1 Peter 2:9), the era has arrived when the people of God are truly becoming ministers.

10. Church leaders are rediscovering the uniqueness of a church's spiritual resources and eternal mission.

Joint Worship Service This Morning Via Webcast: Year 2003

Bellview Baptist Church in Springfield, Missouri held their second annual globalcast via the Web last Sunday morning. This year, they linked up with their fellow missionaries, Jim and Kari Capaldo of Novosibirsk, Russia, for a praise and worship service that was a healthy mix of traditional and contemporary fare.

The service was initiated in prayer, in both English and Russian, and was interpreted simultaneously on the multiple touch-screens provided. As the worship pastors led in prayer, a soft aroma lifted into the air from the SmartSeats that lined the amphitheater from end to end.

The band then started up their instruments in a raucous sound, filled with layer upon layer of digital flutes, guitars, drums, and horns. The whole arena was charged with energy as a vocal team began to sing, starting with a small unrecognizable chant and progressing to a full chorus. A group of foreigners were singing "Holy, Holy, Holy" in their native tongue. In response, those in the youth group were swaying from left to right as they were easily entertained by the fresh rhythms of the singers. Many of the parishioners were led to tears as they viewed the main screen unveiling the interpretation of the song in a continual fluid movement.

I glanced down to the order of service that I downloaded from the church kiosk this morning via my trusty PDA and could not help but notice the historical texts provided from their digital Bible—the lyrics were taken directly from the book of Revelation. A historical book for sure, but a book that looked at the future, just the same.

By the time I looked back up, a host of beautiful holograms featuring different aspects of the world of nature instantaneously appeared across the front of the room. They seemed to capture everyone's attention as the music softened to a more meditative tone over the next several minutes. Up to now, the worship service had a constant ebb and flow of deafening to quiet sounds and dim and bright lighting—all very well orchestrated.

As the music ended, a silence descended on the room. For the first time, I feel a bit uncomfortable. But the morning's speaker shortly replaced the silence. He approached the stage, where a laptop placed on an electronic podium rose up from the floor. He carried nothing with him like the "black book" I was used to seeing only a few years ago when I visited with my friends.

It became apparent that the speaker's entire message and content came from the thin laptop provided him. He seemed very much at ease and very well prepared...enough so that he felt comfortable leaving the stage routinely to ask the audience for input...both from the local audience and the global group in Novosibirsk.

His total interchange with us couldn't have lasted more than 25 minutes, but his communication was clear and concise. Not much fluff. He used everything from movie clips via DVD to holograms of the locations where Jesus supposedly walked.

For an institution that neared virtual extinction at the end of the last century, they seem to finally be catching up with the rest of the world. However, I'll still be looking for the cup holders in the seats...

From House Calls to Mouse Calls

Evangelism in America has taken on a totally new shape. We are no longer in the days of door-to-door visitation techniques. The days of front-porch pleasantries have gone with the wind and the church has been forced to deal with a new deck of cards. The hearts have turned to the joker, and the joker wants the last laugh.

Now, house calls have turned to mouse calls. Today, churches are using entirely new strategies to share the gospel with the world.

Chat rooms are now the virtual hotspot for spreading the good news. People who had become weary of the peering eyes of unknown strangers behind the door are still friendly to those unknown potential friends peering from behind the screen. Today's generation is very much like children at play in the front yard. Any other child who comes by is an automatic potential friend.

On the Web, chat rooms have become the playgrounds of the millennium. We are now seeing the advent of flash-driven tracts, evangelistically laden e-greetings cards, and fireside chat e-mail that shares the gospel story in ways never before seen.

Today's Christians are learning the art of storytelling online. As a result, they are producing their own virtual tracts without all the "Christian malaise." These tracts are real...authentic...persuasive. Imagine the apostle Paul with tenth-generation iMac. You get the picture!

These high-tech evangelists are not folks with a notch-in-the-belt mentality. They are genuine disciples of Jesus the Christ who have a real concern for introducing people to the kingdom of heaven.

The percentage of homes in America with e-mail access has risen to an all time high of 79 percent and continues to increase. Meaning that the digital evangelism revolution still has tremendous room for growth and will likely remain the method of choice for sharing the good news more strategically in the new millennium.

Uirtual Jerusalem: Year 2008

The pastor of Graceway Baptist Church in Springfield, Missouri, asks a newcomer how he met the Lord. His reply startles the pastor: "I met Him at Calvary," he replies dreamily. The pastor responds, "I meant where were you physically when you met Him?" The newcomer replies with impatience, "I already told you: I met Him at Calvary, on my neighbor's virtual reality set. I was the apostle John, and my wife here was Mary. It was incredible. We were walking down the road that led to Calvary. The people on either side of us were yelling at this man dragging a cross on His shoulders. As He passed by, He looked into my eyes, and I saw His love and care for me. It was at that moment that I knew Jesus loved me. My wife and I followed Him to Calvary, and we watched as the soldiers drove the nails into His hands and His feet. We watched Him die for the sins of the world. My wife and I were so moved by this experience that we were compelled to fall on our knees and accept Jesus as our Savior."

While it is true that today's virtual reality graphics hardly rival the richness of God's creation, huge advances in fractal imagery will boost tomorrow's images to rival, perhaps even exceed, the vividness and intricacy of nature. There are some who say that we are in for major changes when computer simulations finally become so realistic that people cannot distinguish them from non-simulated reality.

As the electronic universe expands exponentially, we will experience a radical shift in human history. We are in an expanding electronic universe. At a time when humanity thought it had nothing left to explore, along comes a new frontier with no boundaries or limitations—physical, geographical, logistical, or moral. Instead of suburbs or peaceful countrysides, our future society will inhabit electronic corridors filled with countless artificial enticements. What we now call "cyberspace" and "the electronic superhighway" will soon be called "work," "school," and even "home."

The revolutionary nature of this man-made, alternative reality world will raise a number of ominous issues. People will ask questions like, "What is reality?" and "Why should we prefer this reality?" Perhaps the most frightening question of all will be, "Why not unite with our machines?"

In this environment, the church will be faced with a long list of concerns. Will humanity finally have created a world without God, a world devoid of the Holy Spirit's voice? How do you reach a person who is "living" in an artificial environment not of God's making? What principles of life apply to this artificial universe? How effective is our spiritual armor in this virtual world? And the ultimate question: Will God's sovereignty prevail in cyberspace?

Some people argue that there are significant drawbacks to a lack of personal contact, but the numbers don't lie. There is quantitative evidence that the digital evangelism is producing real converts, and they are joining churches in droves.

Since the advent of the Saddleback Church model in the late twentieth century, membership has become much more clearly defined and deliberately executed in churches today... not leaving much room for the misunderstandings that lead to heresy. Hence, wisdom, knowledge, perseverance, and loyalty are trademark attributes of these newly e-vangelized converts.

The Great Potential

It has been said that the rebirth of American Christianity owes a debt of gratitude to the positive side of the worldwide Web. God is using the development of technology to spread His message of grace and redemption to a generation of technology users who dropped out of church long ago. But serious questions remain: Can we really make genuine disciples online? Will the reliance on communications technology inadvertently obscure our knowledge or proclamation of the Christian message? So far as we can see, the positives clearly have the potential to outweigh the negatives.

6

The Biotech Wave

Science and technology have brought about enormous medical advances and benefits to humanity. The medical field has advanced so fast that some surgeries done even a few years ago are considered primitive. The ability to diagnose, prevent, and treat previous untreatable medical conditions has enriched and saved many lives. These new abilities, however, have opened the door to concerns about how new technologies are being used. Fetal-tissue research, genetic engineering, genetic testing, gene therapy, germline therapy, biopatents, cloning, and reproducing technology all raise complex issues for the Christian. How do we respond to the cloning issue; how should we feel about reproducing technologies? In both biotechnology and bioethics, it is important for Christians to understand the issues and influence the decision-making process at every level.

The question is no longer, "Can we?" because science has now taken the leap from theory to reality. The question is now, "Should we?" Mathematician and Minister John

Polkinhorne, a member of the Human Genetics Advisory Commission in the United Kingdom, wrote:

> Not everything that can be done should be done. The technological imperative, encouraging the continued pioneering of new techniques, must be tempered by the moral imperative, requiring that such techniques should be achieved by ethically acceptable means and employed for ethically acceptable ends. The search for wise decisions must involve the relevant scientific experts (for only they have the access to the knowledge on which the assessments of possibility and consequences can be based), but it cannot be delegated to them alone (for they possess no necessarily unique insight beyond the topic of their professional expertise). There must be other parties in the debate, which centers on the nature of and the respect and restraint due to human life and to human moral dignity. Here theology, with its insight that the good and perfect will of God the Creator is the true origin of all value, has an important contribution to make. Theology will not seek to stifle advances that could benefit humankind in acceptable ways, but will insist that the means by which these desirable ends are achieved must themselves be of ethical integrity.[1]

Theologian Albert Mohler, Jr. made this observation: "Christians should engage in this debate on biblical terms and contend for the sanctity of all created life as well as for the distinction between the creature and the Creator. All technologies, including modern genetics, must be evaluated in terms of the biblical revelation and the totality of the Christian worldview."[2]

Future Wave

Enter Story

Tiger Extinct Since 1936 is Cloned in Zoo: Year 2010

BRIGHTON, Tasmania, Aug. 20, 2010 —A sign by the small enclosure near the Bonorong Park Wildlife Center entrance is inscribed "Tasmanian tiger," but the fabled carnivore is nowhere to be seen. The last known Tasmanian tiger, or *thylacine*, died in captivity in 1936, but a team of Australian biologists believed the animal's extinction was simply an 80-year hiccup. DNA from a Tasmanian tiger had been found, and cloning research began in August of 2000. Hope for the rebirth of the tiger—not a cat at all, but a striped marsupial wolf—lay in the murky depths of a museum specimen jar, where a six-month-old thylacine pup had been preserved in alcohol since 1866.

The Australia Museum director said he knew 15 years earlier that the specimen held the key to the return of the tiger, but it was not until Dolly the sheep was cloned in Scotland in 1997 that technology caught up with his dream.

"It became a matter of not if, but when," the director said.

In April 2000 small samples of heart, liver, muscle, and bone marrow tissue were extracted from the preserved pup, and a small team of evolutionary biologists in Sydney began working to unravel the tiger's genetic code.

Once the DNA damage was assessed and repaired, the tiger's genetic blueprint was inserted into the egg of a close relative, the Tasmanian devil, another marsupial, for incubation.

While there had been similar extinct-animal cloning projects elsewhere in the world, the Australia Museum's project was the first to find good-quality DNA from an extinct specimen.

A far more emotional debate raged over the plan to reincarnate the tiger through cloning. The director had to cross angry picket lines at his museum, and religious groups who accused the scientists of playing God denounced his work.

"My response is that people played God when they exterminated the animal in the first place," said the museum director.

The Biotech Wave Begins

Right about the turn of the century, the third of the five waves of technology kicked in. After a couple false starts in the 1980s and 1990s, biotechnology began to make some real progress toward transforming the medical field. One benchmark came in 2000 with the completion of the Human Genome Project, the effort to map out all human genes. The understanding of our genetic makeup can help lead to a series of breakthroughs in stopping genetic disease.

Whose Genome Is It Anyway? Year 2020

Thank you for considering GenoChoice to plan the future well-being of you and your family. My name is Dr. Elizabeth

Preatner, a prenatal geneticist and embryologist here at GenoChoice. Using our state-of-the-art technologies, you can quite possibly ensure that your child's life may be free of such diseases as cancer, Alzheimer's, and heart disease— as well as conditions like obesity, aggression, and dyslexia.

Our probes and DNA amplifiers can identify the negative genes contributing to these problems and eliminate them in your child...all at the pre-embryonic stage!

And you can even choose specific genes that may help encourage favorable characteristics in your child. With the special help of GenoChoice, you can truly offer your progeny "the best of nature before you nurture!"

This may sound like science fiction to you, but the future of fictional companies like GenoChoice is bright.

The psalmist David might have been looking a few thousand years into the future when he wrote:

> I will praise thee; for I am fearfully and wonderfully made: marvelous are thy works; and that my soul knoweth right well. My substance was not hid from thee when I was made in secret, and curiously wrought in the lowest parts of the earth. Thine eyes did see my substance, yet being unperfect; and in thy book all my members were written, which in continuance were fashioned, when as yet there was none of them (Psalm 139:14-16 KJV).

David acknowledged that God had created him much like a potter who fashions a unique vessel out of clay. God mapped the human genome (pronounced "gee-nome") long before man completed the mapping of the three billion individual "letters" that make up our being. A genome is all the DNA in an organism, including its genes. It's the genes that carry the information for making all the proteins required by all living organisms. These proteins determine many things about the organism—among them are how the organism looks, how well its body metabolizes food or fights infection, and sometimes how it behaves. The order of the DNA underlies all of life's diversity, dictating whether an organism is human or of another species, such as yeast, rice, or fruit fly, all of which have their own distinct genomes and are themselves the focus of individual genome projects.

It began in the Garden of Eden when "God created man in his own image, in the image of God created he him; male and female he created them" (Genesis 1:27). When God created Adam and then took a rib from his side to create Eve, He gave them 24 human chromosomes. These chromosomes determine our individual physical makeup and influence our mental and emotional capacities.

The Human Genome Tsunami

In 1953, Dr. Francis Crick and Dr. James Watson discovered the structure of DNA—the famous double helix. Scientists knew that DNA was the very stuff that life was made of, the material that is passed to children from their parents, and that DNA determines in many respects what they will be as adults and the diseases they might suffer from. During those early days of DNA testing, curiosity and the wish to help alleviate suffering and discover new medicines led to the quest to discover how the genetic information is used by the body. The first stage in such research involved determining the sequence of the genetic information. We've since found that the genetic code is somewhat like binary codes in computers.

Working Together

The project to map the human genome was launched by the U.S. government in 1990. The Human Genome Project (HGP) in the United States, Genethon in France, University of Tokyo Human Genome Center in Japan, and 15 other nations have completed phase one in mapping the Genome. Many private companies, including Celera, Incyte, Geron, Human Genome Sciences, Inc., and Millennium, were involved in a separate mapping effort. The two teams completed the first phase in a tie, after two years of fierce and often bitter competition. The final phase of the human genome-sequencing project will involve deciphering the 3.2 billion DNA letters that make the human body. Researchers are now making the transition from generating a "working draft" of the human DNA to producing the complete "finished" sequence.

This statement appears on the Human Genome Project website:

> The project will reap fantastic benefits for humankind; some that we can anticipate and others that will surprise us....Information generated and technologies developed will revolutionize future biological explorations...medical practices will be radically altered. Emphasis will shift from treatment of the sick to a prevention-based approach....The potential for commercial development presents the U.S. industry with a wealth of opportunity, and sales of biotechnology products are projected to exceed $20 billion by 2001.[3]

Many are saying that this project is the most important scientific endeavor in the last century—far more important that putting a man on the moon or splitting the atom.

Accelerating the Progress

In an achievement compared to Lewis and Clark's mapping of the Louisiana Purchase, two teams of scientists announced on Monday, June 28, 2000 that each had produced a draft version of the human genetic code. The code, also known as the human genome, is the detailed instruction manual for the inner machinery of every member of our species. Scientists believe that having the complete genetic manual will give them a vital tool for fighting disease, maintaining health, and perhaps extending human life.

The joint announcement, which came in a transatlantic news conference held by President Clinton and British Prime Minister Tony Blair, followed weeks of secret negotiations between the leaders of the rival factions: J. Craig Venter, Celera's president and chief scientific officer, and Francis Collins, the leader of the public project.

The ceremony was a moment of shared triumph and an official recognition that a new era in medical science has begun. Clinton, speaking from the East Room of the White House, compared the achievement to the day two centuries ago that Thomas Jefferson met with explorer Meriwether Lewis in the same room to look at the first crude map of the North American continent. The new genetic maps are of "even greater significance," the president said. "Without a doubt, this is the most important, most wondrous map ever produced by humankind."

Clinton and Blair both spoke glowingly of medical advances—of new ways to prevent, diagnose, treat and even cure disease—based on the information contained in the three billion chemical building blocks or letters in the genome. Blair, speaking from 10 Downing Street in London, predicted that the genetic map would bring changes in the first half of the new century as radical as those brought by computer technology in the last half of the past century.

Both leaders, however, expressed concern about the potential for abuse of the new knowledge through genetic discrimination as well as the manipulation of human genetics without a clear understanding of the consequences. "There is no point in arguing whether we're comfortable with it," Blair said. "It's there. It's something we now know. It has the potential to do good."[4]

Both versions of the genome contain numerous gaps and misalignments that could take years to fill and correct; and both competing camps defined—and then redefined—their own finish line for their first, incomplete decoding effort.

Collins, who is director of the National Human Genome Research Institute, pledged that the public effort—carried out at 16 centers in six countries—would continue its work until the job is complete and error-free. That should happen, he said, by 2003, before the fiftieth anniversary of the discovery of the structure of DNA, the staircase-like double helix—the molecule of heredity in all living things.

"It is humbling for me and awe-inspiring to realize that we have caught the first glimpse of our own instruction book, previously known only to God," Collins said. "Historians will consider this a turning point. Researchers in a few years will have trouble imagining how we studied human biology without the genome sequence in front of us."

Collins is also a rare combination of premier scientist and devout Christian. He professes belief in a God that is beyond the reach of science. He says the pursuit of the genetic code is not, as some worry, an attempt by humans to play God, but only mankind's way of admiring God's handi-work.

Venter said that Celera made a point of using samples of DNA from five individuals—three females and two males; Hispanic, Asian, Caucasian, and African American—"out of respect for the diversity that is America, and to help illus-trate that the concept of race has no genetic or scientific basis."[5] The public project used samples of genetic code from a dozen individuals.

A considerable amount of work still remains to be done in completing the genome. Researchers must decipher and list all those chemical letters in order, using samples of DNA contained in all 24 human chromosomes. Large chunks of the genetic code, as much as 10 percent of it, cannot be deci-phered with today's technology. And other smaller pieces will be decoded only over time and with much effort. Like a book with phrases, sentences, and even whole pages missing, there are many gaps that need to be filled.

Dr. Harold Varmus, president of Memorial Sloan-Ket-tering Cancer Center and the former director of National Institutes of Health, says, "We've had genes in hand now for 15 years or so, and we've begun to learn what genes mean one by one. But it's very different to pick a tool out of the toolbox without knowing what else is in there and then sud-denly to know all the tools that are in this toolbox that are used to create a human being. So now we say, 'There are seven screwdrivers and 18 hammers and 15 nails of various kinds.' We know what the instruments are that were neces-sary to make a human being. Let's figure out how to do the hammering and the screwing and the beveling to make a human being, and let's figure out what screws are lost and which have the wrong angle when disease occurs.'"[6]

Dr. Arnold Levine, president of Rockefeller University, said, "What genetics gives us is function. And of course, what the sequence gives us is a book. It's all the words, all the letters in the book, and they're divided into chapters, which could be analogous to chromosomes, for example, and sentences, which could be analogous to meaning, and genes. And to have a complete book all of a sudden makes certain parts of our science really wonderful. It opens up whole new areas for us. I think the human genome sequence and the mouse genome sequence will allow us to do human genetics and allow us to do mouse genetics in a totally new way."[7]

Finishing the mapping process will give scientists, for the first time, the complete DNA, or genetic fingerprint, of one person. Sequencing all of the genes is the first step in this process. Also, once the researchers know the chemicals that make up the genes, they must assemble those chemicals in the proper order. Only then can they tell what the genes do.

What Does the Biotech Wave Hold?

Some have predicted that in the next five to seven years it will be possible to know the genetic causes of a myriad of illnesses, including diabetes, heart disease, multiple sclerosis, and various cancers.

Of course, the knowledge gleaned from mapping the human genome will lead to many ethical questions. One benefit is that people could be tested for prospective future illnesses and possibly take drugs or alter their lifestyles to avoid or delay the onset of those illnesses. But one danger is that people might avoid taking such tests if they lead to discrimination in employment or health insurance decisions. Scientists are urging the U.S. Congress to pass "effective legislation to prevent genetic discrimination" in health insurance and employment, noting that several "carefully crafted bills" on the issues had already been submitted.

Among other things, the genome findings could make it possible to screen children for hundreds of diseases before birth. Genes for an enormous range of traits, such as eye and hair color, height, intelligence, and longevity, may also be known.

It is unlikely a patent will be issued on the gene for a particular eye color. President Clinton and British Prime Minister Tony Blair both agree that no one should own such information. However, the process for changing a child's eye color from green to brown could be subject to patent. And though the gene for a disease such as cystic fibrosis could not be patented, the therapies developed to treat the disease could be.

A quick glance around any public gathering attests to the physical diversity of the human population. In most groups of people, some will be tall, others short; some will have brown eyes, and others blue. A person's genes—packets of the genetic material DNA, which make up chromosomes in the human cell—largely determine his or her physical attributes, such as height, complexion, and hair and eye color.

As scientists begin to map and analyze the molecular details of the complete set of human genes, will it matter whose genes they use? In many ways, describing the anatomy of the human genome will be similar to studying the human heart or the human brain. While there are small differences from person to person in the size and shape of these organs, most of the key characteristics are the same. Although human beings are distinct from one another, they are really very similar in most biologically important respects. That's what makes us human. So the map of the human genome can be based on information collected from many different people, and most of the information in that map will pertain to everyone.

The tiny differences between any two people rest in only two to ten million (out of the three billion total) nucleotide bases, an amount that computes to about 1 percent or less of their total DNA. Because these small differences vary from person to person, it doesn't matter whose genes are used for the research work.

Eventually, scientists will "map" or establish the distinctive genetic landmarks from one end of a chromosome to the other, and add that information to the genetic map of the entire human genome. This complete map will become the "reference" to which researchers will compare DNA taken from a variety of people as scientists look for disease genes and other important genetic regions located on chromosomes. A particular region on a chromosome, for example, may be found to contain information about height. Although the genetic content of that specific site may change slightly from person to person, the location of the site will be the same in each person's genome.

Because studying the entire six-foot stretch of human DNA is a huge project, scientists are tackling the genome one chromosome at a time. Even then, analyzing the information in just one chromosome is an enormous task for a single research group. That's why many scientists have been assigned only portions of a chromosome at a time. The complete map for a single chromosome will then be derived from samples collected from several unrelated people by researchers in many different laboratories.

When asked about the future of the Genome Project, Francis Collins, the project's director, said, "We needed brain power to come up with the technical solutions that allowed us to reduce the cost of sequencing from $10 a letter down to four cents a letter, which is where we are right now. That doesn't happen without a huge amount of engineering, robotics, physics, chemistry, biology, and gel electrophoresis expertise getting together and solving that problem." He continues:

> But, where we need to go from here is a whole pro-
> liferation of new disciplines aimed at understanding
> these three billion base pairs, aimed at under-
> standing how, even though you have the same DNA
> in your liver cell and your muscle cell, genes are
> turning on and off in very different ways in those
> two locations.
>
> They have the same instructions. How does the cell
> know which ones to use and which ones to keep
> silent? That enterprise, which we used to look at one
> gene at a time, in a very slow, painful process—you
> can now look at all of them at once because we've got
> the genome essentially in front of us.
>
> How do we figure out of the proteins that these
> genes code for—what do they do? Where are they in
> the cell? Which ones touch each other and activate
> each other in certain ways? Again, we used to do that
> one protein at a time. It took a whole career just to
> study one protein. We're too impatient. We're not
> going to do that anymore. Now it has to be done
> with a genomic attitude.
>
> Biology and medicine has taken on a genomic atti-
> tude in subtle ways over the last few years. There's
> no turning back. This instruction book will make
> the study of human biology available to everybody.
> And you won't ask questions or answer them in the
> same tired, old way that we used to be stuck with.
>
> We're going to find the answers to those killer dis-
> eases and malfunctions that have done so much
> damage to us. And that is virtually every disease.
> There is no disease, except some cases of trauma,
> that doesn't have hereditary contributions. That

means that within this mysterious DNA molecule, we will find the clues to what those diseases are really all about. There will be no exceptions. This is not a strategy that's going to leave out a long list of disorders because they didn't turn out to benefit from it. It will be directly applicable to whatever it is that runs in my family or yours and that may ultimately cause us to become ill. The consequences of this are global, in the medical sense. They're not limited to one set of disorders.[8]

Wakeup Call from the Biological Clock: Year 2023

At the close of the twentieth century, technology had become nothing short of the god of civilization. Today, technology's "miraculous" advances are commonplace. What was once extraordinary is now ordinary.

However, as a result, it seems we have given rise to a new god. . . biology. The blending and blurring of the lines that distinguish the two make them practically invisible today.

The first cyborg was born over 65 years ago, in 1958, when the first pacemaker was installed. Life as we know it received its first upgrade...or did it? The day science dabbled with the DNA pool was the time for the lifeguard to dive in, but no lifeguard was found. Christianity was silent, and

woke up too late to play lifeguard to a generation fasci-
nated with fabrication. So when Christendom finally
decided to step up to the edge of the genetic pool and
throw out a line, it got nothing in return but the backside
wake of a culture gone wild.

Parents now have their pick of the litter, and chose to litter
the petri dish with the parental leftovers. While parishioners picketed the abortion clinics, the mad scientists
were at work on the maniacal that would soon overshadow
anything seen before.

The question Christendom must now ask is this: Can it
break into the biological realm and not be made a laughing-
stock? Can Christians make a difference in DNA dabbling?

Tragically, near the end of the twentieth century, many
Bible colleges died out or converted to a more holistic
approach to spirituality. However, a few steadfast schools
have given us a new generation of believers with a bent for
the biological. What many leaders in Christendom missed
in recent decades is that holistic biblical teaching applied to
the arts and sciences is what could have equipped the
church to stay in step with what has been happening in the
scientific world.

Medical ethics has become the political hot potato now,
and we are long overdue for a real-time engagement of
Christianity and biology. Will the church stand up? That
remains to be seen, but there is evidence that believers are
stepping up and speaking out. Come on church, the time
is now!

What Does God Think?

When asked, "Where is God in all this?" Dr. Collins replied: "God is not threatened by all this, I'm happy to report. I think God thinks it's wonderful that we puny creatures are about the business of trying to understand how our instruction book works, because it's a very elegant instruction book indeed. And, as somebody whose faith is important to him, I actually find it rather rewarding to be engaged in a process of understanding something about human biology that God understood all along."[9]

Someone then asked Dr. Collins if it was possible to use information about the human genome in order to wipe out only certain kinds of people.

"They might find out they've wiped out their own family," said Dr. Collins. "When you look at the differences between us, 99.9 percent are actually differences you find in every ethnic group, from every origin. So the ability to be able to choose a particular DNA variant and say, 'Well, I'm going to use that one to wipe out the people I don't like'— scientifically, that isn't plausible. That's because we all descended from a common pool of genetic coding that originated with Adam."

How Fast Will the Research Go?

Dr. Collins predicted that within ten years, doctors would be able to tell patients whether they have genes that make them susceptible to such diseases as high blood pressure, diabetes, and heart disease. "That kind of predictive information could be quite useful to you...because it would allow you to practice individualized preventive medicine focusing on the things that are most important for your own health," he said. In 15 to 20 years, he predicted, it might be possible for doctors to prescribe drugs targeted directly at genes and their protein products.

Scientists know that they are decades away from fully comprehending the DNA text. Still, they promise a new era of medicine with new treatments for nearly every medical ailment—treatments that come from tweaking the genes that tell cells how to go about the work of daily life.

For example, instead of poisoning a cancer patient with chemotherapy, doctors might simply tell the genes inside tumor cells that it is time to die. Instead of giving clotting factors to hemophiliacs, doctors might fix a patient's flawed genes as though they were changing a broken gasket on a car. Dozens of other ailments could be eased or cured as researchers invent drugs that tell certain genes to work harder or other genes to stop working altogether.

"This genome sequence is really going to create revolutionary change in everything associated with human health," said Richard Young, a gene researcher and biology professor at the Massachusetts Institute of Technology. "It will range from a better understanding of basic biology to new diagnostic tests for the major health problems to new cures for disease."[10]

No one can predict exactly when an automated system will be ready to scan anyone's genome in search of clues about disease. But that day is sure to come, scientists say. A drop of blood will probably be all that's necessary to supply enough material for such a machine, which would then spit out a list of each patient's inborn disease susceptibilities and strengths.

Once genetic diagnosis is readily available—and relatively inexpensive—it will offer an extraordinarily powerful tool for use in the medical clinic. Gene analysis should be able to warn years in advance about someone's potential for genetic ailments or diseases. The complex interactions of the genes involved in heart disease and cancer, for example, may become "readable" long before problems ever strike.

According to biologist Richard Young, highly specialized electronic chips—similar to the integrated circuits now found in the innards of computers—have been devised for "gene-reading." Samples of someone's DNA can be spread onto the surface of such a chip, and tiny lights, fluorescent areas, begin glowing to pinpoint which genes are active, and which are turned on.[11] Such chips, made by Affymetrix Inc. and other companies, enable scientists to see how genes operate during the progression of a disease.

Progress in Health Care

Lawrence Lehman, M.D., a physician with two decades of experience in academic clinical medicine, medical administration, medical publishing, and managed healthcare, recently said:

> Medically, the next two decades will be remembered most for the prolongation in high-quality life expectancy and aging; explosive growth in biotechnology; the implementation of universal healthcare coverage; and the increased percentage of GDP spent on healthcare and pharmaceuticals.

> By 2020, quality life expectancies will have increased by 20 years or longer, introducing an array of compelling societal and sociological issues. Age groups ("Boomers" vs. "X-ers") will compete as each strives to maintain jobs and relative income and socioeconomic levels. An increasingly aged population will place enormous and unexpected pressures on the Social Security and Medicare systems, delaying retirement, for most, to the mid-70s and beyond. New markets for technology and luxury items to

support a wealthy class of educated, productive, and experienced older workers will develop.

The biotech explosion will occupy the front pages for decades to come. Virtually all chronic medical and surgical conditions will be found to either have a genetic basis, a genetic sensitivity subject to therapeutic manipulation, or an infectious etiology treatable by new classes of pharmaceuticals. All diagnostic studies will be noninvasive; many will involve use of nanochip technology probes; almost all therapeutic interventions will also be minimally invasive, replacing conventional surgery.

Preventative cocktails of neutraceuticals, pharmaceuticals, genes, and nanochips will be as commonplace as today's vitamin supplements. Traditional academic medical centers will be replaced by "centers of excellence" concentrating on specific diseases and treatments. Evidence-based, outcome-driven protocols and best-practices guidelines will replace today's empirical approaches. Telemedicine, telesurgery, and distance learning will transform the traditional hospital and academic medical center.

The pharmaceutical industry will be regulated closely by the federal government to assure fair access and fair pricing of drugs and therapeutics. The federal government will also oversee universal healthcare coverage. Basic health care will be considered a right; but superior care will be regarded as a luxury for which individuals will be willing to allocate considerable disposable income to "buy up" to a variety of premium and luxury packages. Marquis health care will be perceived as a status symbol. As health care directly competes for disposable income with commercial goods and services, entertainment, and technology, health care will rise from 15 percent GDP now to 20 percent in 2020.

The next 20 years will welcome a significant prolongation of human life, productivity, and progress as biotechnology fuses with information technology. The ever-increasing availability of information and knowledge about disease and the ability to alter the course and natural history of many common diseases genetically and pharmaceutically will have a radical positive effect on human life.[12]

Routine Checkup: Year 2020

The routine physical exam has changed considerably since the time it was likened to a mechanic who diagnosed your car by listening to the engine. If the engine was purring smoothly, the mechanic said the car was perfectly fine. But internally the car could have been on the verge of a major breakdown. Similarly, a physical exam consisting of rudimentary tests on your body, such as taking a blood sample and checking your blood pressure, could not tell the doctor what was happening at the genetic and molecular level. Even after a thorough medical checkup with an electrocardiogram, you could still walk out of the doctor's office and drop dead on the floor with a heart attack.

By contrast, a physical exam now involves checking your personalized DNA sequence. Your doctor will take a blood sample and send it to a genetics laboratory. Within a month, he will have a CD that contains your complete DNA sequence. This will help determine whether you have any of the 5,000 known genetic diseases. After reviewing your personalized DNA sequence, your doctor will be able to predict with accuracy the mathematical chances of your getting any number of diseases. He can then give you preventive measures, possibly even years before any symptom arises. Your personalized DNA is now the foundation on which your health is analyzed.

Understanding the Human Genome

Here are some important interesting facts related to the human genome:

- The genome contains the biological instruction for how an individual is formed and how the cells in the body function.

- Except for identical twins, the gene structure is unique in each individual.

- Half of the genes in a person come from each parent.

- Genes direct the formation, or expression, of proteins that a cell uses to function, repair, or defend itself, and to divide.

- Genes are contained in the chromosomes in the nucleus of each cell.

- There are 22 numbered chromosomes, plus two that determine gender, X and Y.

- A female has two X chromosomes, while a male has an X and a Y.

- A human normally has 23 pairs of chromosomes.

- A complete human genome is contained in a coiled double helix of DNA, or deoxyribonucleic acid. Stretched out, the coil would be 6 feet long, but only 20 microns wide. A human hair is about 50 microns wide.

- About three billion DNA subunits, called base pairs, make up the double helix.

- Most of the base pairs of DNA between genes have no known function. These base pairs are commonly referred to as "junk DNA." Genes give coded instructions to the cell on how to assemble proteins.

- The making of a protein from this code is called "gene expression." Many human disorders are caused by genetic flaws, or by the absence of one or more genes.

Biotech and Agriculture

The biotech revolution is profoundly affecting another economic sector—agriculture. The deeper understanding we are gaining of genetics leads us to breed plants more precisely. In the next decade, much produce in the United States will be genetically engineered by these new techniques. The same applies to livestock. In 1997, the cloning of sheep in the United Kingdom startled the world and kicked off a flurry of activity in this field, which includes the genetic tweaking of prize livestock to the benefit of growers. As well, research continues on raising animals whose organs can be donated to humans. All this is happening with the goal of cultivating superproductive animals and ultra-hardy, high-yielding plants that can bring a green revolution to countries with large populations.

How Far Will Biotechnology Take Us?

Just how far will biotechnology take us, and how far should we let this future wave take us? Leonard Sweet (www. leonardsweet.com) said it best:

> God gave spiritual navigators a plumb line. There are design limits to creativity. The line on the ship is called the Plimsoll line.
>
> Sea-vessel captains take pains to watch a hull marking called the Plimsoll line. More and more things can be added to the boat as long as the water level remains below the Plimsoll line. When the level is reached, the boat has taken on too much cargo and is in danger of sinking. No matter how much rearrangement takes place on board ship, the problem is the carrying capacity itself, which has been breached. Either one respects the Plimsoll line, or one is sunk. To go over the Plimsoll Point is to go beyond the point of no return. In a storm, to save the ship that went beyond the Plimsoll line, sailors often cast cargo overboard. The most famous of cargos to be cast overboard was Jonah.
>
> Spiritual leaders will need to be wisdomized to get at least one jump ahead of the field—and sometimes two—to show to this culture its Plimsoll Points.
>
> • It's OK—bring on board genetic engineering to enhance agriculture and ignite a second green revolution.

- It's OK—load up biotechnology that can create bug-resistant potatoes, apples, pears, and other fruits.

- It's OK—transgenic beets, even parrots that can withstand cold North American temperatures.

- It's OK—take one organism's DNA and insert it into another, like beetatoes.

But combine the genes of the human species with plants or animals? You've gone beyond the Plimsoll Point.

- It's safe. Tinker with the DNA to eliminate almost 2,000 thousand single-gene diseases, such as Huntington's Chorea.

- It's safe. Manipulate DNA to reduce the diseases with genetic predispositions, such as dozens of cancers.

But take nuclei from the cells of mature humans, and use them to produce children? You've gone beyond the Plimsoll Point.

Human cloning in the quest of immortality? Past the Plimsoll Point.

Many scientists and physicists are saying that by 2040 it will be possible for people to routinely scan their brains into a computer and create self-replicas. Even if the technology makes it possible, should we "mindcopy" the brain electronically, bit by bit, connection by connection, synapse by synapse, neuron by neuron to create a nanotechnological body?

You've reached the Plimsoll Point.[13]

Who Are We Doing It For?

The potential of improving and extending the quality of human life in the future is amazing indeed. Advancements in medical technology are part of the biblical "cultural mandate." Mankind is endowed by its Creator with the potential of using human intelligence in order to rule this world for God. The only real question is whether we will do it for God…or for ourselves.

7

The Nanotechnology Wave

Nanotechnology is an emerging science that deals with our world on the molecular level, atom by atom, molecule by molecule. It is a technology that will allow us to manipulate the smallest building blocks of matter. Starting from these small building blocks will allow us to build large objects, some we can't even imagine today. The only reason that building devices from such small parts is being taken seriously by IBM, Xerox, and other technology powerhouses is because of a phenomenon known as self-assembly. Scientists say that if you lay down the proper sort of base structure, you can "grow" nanotubes, nanospheres, and nanotransistors for computers. Today, billions of dollars are being spent on research, and breakthroughs in the field indicate that nanotech, or small-scale engineering, is a serious endeavor—one that has the potential to realign global economies.

Making Progress with Nanotechnology

By 2020, scientists and engineers will likely have figured out reliable methods of constructing objects one atom at a time.

Products of nanotech will be all around us, impacting our lives and changing the way we live. Among the first commercially viable products are likely to be tiny sensors that can enter a person's bloodstream and bring back information about its composition. By 2018, these micromachines might be able to do basic cell repair. In addition, nanotechnology promises to have a profound impact on traditional manufacturing as the century rolls on. Theoretically, most goods could be produced much more efficiently through nanotech techniques. By 2025, the theory will still be far from proven, but by that time we may see small desktop factories for producing simple products.

Eventually, nanotechology will begin to be applied to the development of computing at the atomic level. Quantum computing, rather than DNA computing, may prove to be the heir to microprocessors in the short run. In working up to the billion-transistor microprocessor, engineers will probably hit insurmountable technical barriers: the scale of integrated circuits will have shrunk so small that optical-lithography techniques will fail to function. Only when quantum computing is developed will increases in computing power once again promise to continue unabated for the foreseeable future.

By 2020, nanotech could become a multitrillion dollar industry, and even then it will still be in its embryonic stages. Once nanotech is understood and harnessed, it will enable us to create anything that presently exists, as well as unimaginable new things.

For example, we could create micromachines that are able to repair our body's cells or organs. Submicron-size biochips could possibly be deployed to bring drugs to the human body exactly where they're needed. We may be able to use nanotechnology to attack viruses and neutralize the triggering devices for cancer or AIDS. Tiny nanolabs might be able to create energy by rearranging common molecules. Diamonoids—material as strong as diamonds—are already on the drawing board. These diamonoids will be used for repairing bones and teeth so they never break or deteriorate.

As we place intelligence into these new sensors and microchips and then embed them into objects around us, these objects will be able to communicate with us. For example, our clothes may be able to warn us of danger. Or, they may be able to detect that they are getting smaller or larger as we lose or gain weight.

Life in the Nano-lane: Year 2020

Mindy wakes up startled. Though it is the middle of summer outside with temperatures rising to the mid-90s, her room is engulfed in a wintry snow scene from the Himalayas in India. She had downloaded the program from the global brain, but had not chosen this particular setting for this morning. She was expecting to wake up on the shores of Maui with a dazzling sunrise. "Engage Maui program," she orders. Suddenly her room is transported into the steamy jungles of South America, somewhere in Brazil. "What's this? Travel bot off!" she orders, frustrated that her morning was ruined by this new technology. Her virtual-world bedroom returns to normal.

Mindy orders her personal net agent to look into the problem. She thinks the command, *fix now,* and her agent immediately springs into action, contacting the Virtual

World vendor. Within a few minutes the diagnosis comes in. "The program needed an upgrade," says her lifestyle agent. "Well, at least my nano-device won't need an upgrade," Mindy says to herself. Just last week Mindy had the nano-implant embedded just below her right temple. The device is smaller than a pinhead and allows her brain to plug into her smart house, computer, and the global brain. Voice, eye, and thought commands give her 24-hour access to anyone and any information in the universe.

As she walks down the hallway into the living room and then into the kitchen, intelligent sensors embedded into the walls, light fixtures, floor, and a number of other places wake up and start to communicate to her. These nanosensors are learning about her and are sensing what she needs for comfort and health in her home.

Because Mindy woke up this morning with a headache, she takes two nanobios. They are pain-suppressants that are personalized and programmed to analyze and cure her headache in real time. Within eight seconds her headache is gone. She is ready to start her day.

The Benefits of Nanotechnology

Saving the Earth

All four waves of technology—computers, telecom, biotech, and nanotech—are contributing to a new surge of economic activity. In the past, in the industrial era, a booming economy usually put a severe strain on the environment because almost everything we made created a lot of waste by-products. The logic of the era also tended toward larger and larger factories, which created more and more pollution.

Biotech, on the other hand, doesn't create as much waste by-product. It also emulates the processes of nature, creating much less pollution. Infotech, which moves information electronically rather than physically, also makes much less of an environmental impact on the natural world. Moving information across the United States through the relatively simple infotechnology of fax machines, for example, is seven times more energy-efficient than sending it through Federal Express. Furthermore, these information technologies are constantly being refined, with each new generation of equipment becoming more and more energy efficient, with lower and lower environmental impact. However, there is one more technology being developed that may provide the answer we need.

Alternative Energy

The fifth wave of new technology—alternative energy—is arriving with the introduction of the hybrid electric car. Stage one of this wave began in the late 1990s when automobile companies such as Toyota rolled out vehicles using small diesel- or gasoline-fueled internal-combustion engines to power an onboard generator that then drives small electric motors at each wheel. The car runs on electric power at low RPMs but uses the internal-combustion engine at highway speeds, avoiding the problem of completely battery-powered electric vehicles that run out of juice after 60 miles. The early hybrids are also much more efficient than regular gas-powered cars, often getting as much as 80 miles to a gallon.

Stage two is likely to be spurred by aerospace companies such as Allied Signal, which will use their knowledge of jet engines to build hybrids powered by gas turbines. In time, technology previously confined to an aircraft's onboard electric systems may successfully migrate to automobiles. These cars will use natural gas to power the onboard generators, which in turn will drive the electric motors at the wheels. They will also make use of superstrong, ultra-light new materials that take the place of steel and allow big savings on gas mileage.

Ideally, the third and final stage would be hybrids that use hydrogen fuel cells. Hydrogen is the simplest and most abundant atom in the universe, and it would make a great source of power for electric generators, with the only waste product being water. No exhaust, no carbon monoxide—just water. The basic tenets of this hydrogen-power technology were developed as far back as the Apollo space program, but then it was still extremely expensive, and explosions were a recurring problem. By the late 1990s, research labs such as British Columbia-based Ballard Power Systems were steadily making progress with this technology with little public fanfare. Eventually we could see transitional hydrogen cars that extract fuel from ordinary gasoline. After that, hydrogen could be processed in refinery-like plants and put into cars that can go thousands of miles—and many months—before refueling. Such technology would be vastly cheaper and safer than what we have today.

These technological developments could bring about a wholesale transformation of the automobile industry through the first quarter of the new century. Initially the automakers were forced to make better cars because of government decrees, such as California's zero-emission mandate—which called for 10 percent of new cars by 2003 to have zero emissions. But the new technology now arising, which likely will include hybrid cars, will bring a surge in car sales not because the hybrids are the environmentally correct option but because they're sporty, fast, and fun. The auto companies will build them because executives see green—as in money, not trees.

With such a change, the automobile industry will need to completely retool its factories, which could send reverberations throughout the global economy over a ten- to fifteen-year period. At the same time, the petrochemical giants will need to begin switching from maintaining vast networks that bring oil from remote Middle Eastern deserts to building similarly vast networks that will supply the nation with the new elements of electrical power. Fossil fuels will continue to be a primary source of power into the middle of the twenty-first century, but they will be clean fossil fuels. And almost all new cars will be hybrid vehicles that use hydrogen power. That development alone will defuse much of the pressure on the global environment. As a result, the world may be able to support quite a few additional automobile drivers after all.

8

The Globalization Wave

Earlier, we discovered how the end of the Cold War has helped to initiate the waves of technology rippling through our world today. But that's only half the story. The other half has to do with an equally powerful force: globalization. While our world is being spurred forward by new technologies, the emergence of an interconnected planet is being propelled more by the power of an idea—the idea of an open society.

Asia has several countries that are economic powerhouses in their own right. India has built on its top-notch technical training and mastery of the lingua franca of the high-tech world, English, to challenge many Western countries in software development. Malaysia's audacious attempt to jump-start an indigenous high-tech sector through massive investments in a multimedia supercorridor has paid off. And we all know Japan's dominant position as a producer of technological goods. In the space of one full 80-year lifespan, Asia has gone from almost uninterrupted poverty to widespread wealth.

From a historical vantage point, globalization began around 1980. One individual who articulated well the idea of an open society was Mikhail Gorbachev. It's Gorbachev who helped bring about some of its most dramatic manifestations: the fall of the Wall, the collapse of the Soviet empire, and the end of the Cold War. He helped initiate a vast wave of political changes that included the democratization of Eastern Europe and Russia. To kick it off, Gorbachev introduced two key concepts to the Politburo in 1985—two ideas that resonated not just in the Soviet Union but also through the entire world. One was *glasnost*, the other, *perestroika*. Openness and restructuring—the formula for the age, the key ingredients of the future wave.

A Civilization of Civilizations

We're forming a new civilization, a global civilization, distinct from those that arose before this era. It's not just Western civilization forcing itself on others. It's not a resurgent Chinese civilization struggling to reassert itself after years of being thwarted. It's a strange blend of both, and the others. It's something different, something still being born. By 2020, information technologies will have spread to every corner of the planet. Real-time language translation will likely be possible. The great cross-fertilization of ideas—the ongoing, never-ending planetary conversation—has begun. From this, the new crossroads of all civilizations, the new civilization will emerge.

In many ways, it's a civilization of civilizations. We're building a framework that will enable all the world's civilizations to exist side by side and thrive—where the best attributes of each can stand out and make their unique contributions, where the peculiarities of each are cherished and allowed to live on. We're entering an age where diversity is truly valued—the more options, the better. Our ecosystem works best that way. Our market economy works best that way. Our civilization, the realm of our ideas, works best that way, too. But will the powers-that-be allow this to continue?

The Millennial Generation

We may now be seeing the world begin going through a changeover in power. This changeover could happen not through force, but through natural succession—a generational transition. The aging baby boomers, born in the wake of World War II, will eventually fade from their prominent positions of economic and moral leadership. The tough-minded, techno-savvy generation that trails them, the digital generation, has the new world wired. But these two generations have simply laid the groundwork, preparing the foundations for the civilization that comes next.

The millennial generation is now coming of age. These are the children born in the 1980s and 1990s, at the front end of this boom of all booms. These are the kids who have spent their entire lives steeped in the new technologies, living in a networked world. They have been educated in wired schools; they have taken their first jobs implicitly understanding computer technologies. Now they're doing the bulk of society's work. They are comprising more and more of the work force and turning their attention to the next generation of problems that remain to be cracked.

These are higher-level concerns, the intractable problems—such as eradicating poverty on the planet—which people throughout history have believed impossible to solve. This generation has witnessed an extraordinary spread of prosperity across the planet, so they see no inherent barrier keeping them from extending that prosperity to—why not?—everyone. Then there's the environment. The millennial generation has inherited a planet that's in serious shape. Now comes the difficult problem of restoration, starting with the rain forests. Then there's governance. Americans will soon vote electronically from home, but e-voting will just be an extension of the 250-year-old system of liberal democracy. Interactive technologies may soon bring about radically new forms of participatory democracy on a scale never imagined. Many young people say that the end of the nation-state is in sight.

These ambitious projects will not be solved in a decade, or two, or even three. But the lifespan of this generation will stretch across the entire twenty-first century. Given the state of medical science, many members of the millennial generation will live 100 years. Over the course of their lifetimes, they will confidently foresee the solutions to many seemingly intractable problems. And they will fully expect to see some big surprises. Almost certainly there will be significant, unexpected breakthroughs in the realm of science and technology. What will be the twenty-first century's equivalent of the discovery of the electron or DNA? What strange new ideas will emerge from the collective mind of billions of brains wired together all over the planet?

Learning from the Past

What we're describing is only a scenario of the future. By no means are we making outright predictions of what is to come. We can be reasonably confident, however, of the continuation of certain trends. For example, much of the future-waves technology is already in motion and is still on the rise. Asia is ascending, and barring some bizarre catastrophe, that large portion of the world will continue to grow exponentially. But there are many unknowns, all kinds of critical uncertainties. Will Europe summon the political will to make the transition to the new economy? Will Russia avoid a return to nationalist ways and establish a healthy market economy—let alone democracy? Will China fully embrace capitalism and avoid causing a new cold—or hot—war? Will a rise in terrorism cause the world to pull back in constant fear? It's not technology or economics that pose the biggest challenges to the future wave. It's political factors, the ones dependent on strong leadership.

One hundred years ago, the world went through a similar process of technical innovation and unprecedented economic integration that led to a global boom. New transportation and communications technologies—railroads, telegraphs, and telephones—spread all over the planet, enabling a coordination of economic activity at a level never seen before. Indeed, the 1890s have many parallels to the 1990s—for better or worse. The potential of new technologies appeared boundless. An industrial revolution was spurring social and political revolution. It couldn't be long, it seemed, before a prosperous, society arrived; it was a wildly optimistic time.

Of course, it all ended in catastrophe. The leaders of the world increasingly focused on narrow national agendas. The nations of the world broke from the path of increasing integration and lined up in competing factions. The result was World War I, with everyone using the new technologies to wage bigger, more efficient, and more devastating war. After the conflict, the continued pursuit of nationalist agendas severely punished the losers and consolidated colonial empires. The world went from wild optimism to—quite literally—depression in a very short time.

The lessons of World War I contrast sharply with those of World War II. The move toward a closed economy and society after the first war led to global fragmentation as nations pulled back on themselves. In the aftermath of

World War II, the impetus was toward an open economy and society—at least in half of the world. This led down a path of continuing integration. Many world leaders had the foresight to establish an array of international institutions to help facilitate the emerging global economy. They worked hard to rebuild their vanquished enemies, Germany and Japan, through generous initiatives like the Marshall Plan. This philosophical shift from closed to open societies came about through bold leadership, much of it coming from the United States. In the wake of World War I, American political and business leaders embraced isolationism, with severe consequences for the world. After World War II, they did the opposite, with very different results.

A Crucial Responsibility

Today, the United States has a similarly crucial leadership role to play. There are purely practical reasons for this. The United States has the single largest economy in the world, a market with a big influence on the flow of world trade. It has the biggest research and scientific establishment by far. Since the demise of the Soviet Union, no other country has possessed a comparable array of university research facilities, corporate industrial labs, and nonprofit think tanks. The combination of a huge economy and a scientific elite also gives the United States the world's strongest military; the country can develop the weapons and pay the bills. For the next decade or so, at the very least, America will be the preeminent military power. These reasons alone ensure that the United States, regardless of the intentions of its leaders, will have a huge influence on any future scenario. But the role of the United States is more involved, more complicated than that.

The United States is the great innovator nation, the incubator of new ideas. Just as the new technologies of the early

Industrial Revolution were born in England, the vast majority of innovations in the computer and telecommunications fields are happening now in the United States. Americans are fundamentally shaping the core technologies and infrastructure that will be at the foundation of the twenty-first century. Partly because of that, the United States is the first country to transition to the new economy. American corporations have been the first to adopt the new technologies and adapt to the changing economic realities. As a nation, the United States is figuring out how to finesse the new model of high economic growth driven by new technologies. The American people are feeling the first social and cultural effects. And the American government is the first to feel the strain that comes with change. The United States is paving the way for other developed nations and, eventually, the rest of the world.

Even more important is the fact that the United States serves as steward of the idea of an open society. The United States is home to the core economic and political values that emerged from the twentieth century—the free-market economy and democracy. But the idea of an open society is broader than that. Americans believe in the free flow of ideas, products, and people. Historically, this has taken the form of protecting speech, promoting trade, and welcoming immigrants. With the coming of a wired, global society, the concept of openness has never been more important. It's the linchpin that will make the new world work.

The United States, as first among equals, needs to live this concept in the coming decades. One of the great tasks before us is integrating the former communist adversaries China and Russia into the world community in much the same way that Japan and Germany were integrated after World War II. This is the main geopolitical challenge of the new century. Then there's the need to create a complex fabric of new global economic and political institutions to fit the twenty-first century. Though these need not take the bureaucratic shape they did in the past, a certain level of the coordination of global activities will continue to fall in the public sphere. We spent decades in excruciating negotiations to disarm and limit nuclear proliferation. But now we are in an age of information warfare, and we face a very different set of security concerns and a laborious process to find global solutions.

The vast array of problems to solve and the sheer magnitude of the changes that need to take place are enough to make any global organization give up, any nation back down, any reasonable person curl up in a ball. That's where Americans have one final contribution to make: optimism, that maddening can-do attitude that doesn't accept limits. Americans have boundless confidence in their ability to solve problems. And they have an amazing capacity to think they really can change the world.

Yes, a global transformation over the next quarter century inevitably will bring a tremendous amount of trauma. The world will run into an incredible number of problems as we transition to a networked economy and a global society. Apparent progress will be followed by setbacks. And all along the way the chorus of doomsayers will insist it simply can't be done. But the determination of those who drive the process of change can help to keep the world moving forward rather than backward.

The Global Stampede

By the close of the twentieth century, the more-developed Western nations were forging ahead on a path of technology-led growth, and booming Asia was showing the unmistakable benefits of developing market economies and free trade.

In this new millennium, the path for the rest of the world seems clear: openness and restructuring. Individually, nations that want to keep up will begin adopting the formula of deregulating, privatizing, opening up to foreign investment, and cutting government deficits. Collectively, they will sign onto international agreements that accelerate the process of global integration—and fuel the long boom.

Two milestones came in 1997: the Information Technology Agreement (IT), in which almost all participating countries agree to abolish tariffs by 2000, and the Global Telecommunications Accord, in which almost 70 leading nations agree to rapidly deregulate their domestic telecom markets. These two developments are now quickening the spread of the two key technologies of the era: computers and telecommunications.

Everyone benefits from IT, particularly the underdeveloped economies, which are able to leapfrog upward to the newest, cheapest, best technology rather than settling for obsolete junk. IT creates a remarkable dynamic that brings increasing power, performance, and quality to each new generation of the technology—plus big drops in price. Also, wireless telecommunications enable poorer countries to keep up with the rest of the world without having to expend the huge cost and effort of building wired infrastructures through crowded cities and distant countrysides.

This all bodes well for the world economy, with one exception: the Middle East. In many Arab countries, the fundamentalist Muslim mind-set is not receptive to the fluid demands of the digital age. The new economy rewards experimentation, constant innovation, and challenging the status quo. These attributes, however, are shunned in many places throughout the Middle East, where many people become more firmly entrenched in past traditions in response to the furious pace of change. Also, the advent of hydrogen power could eventually undermine the centrality of oil in the world economy. If the auto industry converted to hydrogen power, the bottom could fall out of the oil market. This, in turn, could lead to a crisis. Would the people then insist on change from the old monarchies and religious regimes? Could this bring about a war in the Middle East?

Future Aftershocks

Riding the wave of the booming economy brings other major social and political repercussions. Inevitably, fundamental shifts in technology and the means of production will bring changes in the way the economy operates. And when the economy changes, it doesn't take long for the rest of society to adapt to the new realities. The classic example is the transformation of agricultural society into industrial society. A new tool (the motor) led to a new economic model (capitalism) that brought great social upheaval (urbanization and the creation of an affluent class), and ultimately profound political change (liberal democracy). While that's a crude summation of a complex historical transition, the same dynamic largely holds true in our shift to a networked economy based on digital technologies.

There's also a commonsense explanation. When an economy booms, money courses through society, people get rich quick, and almost everybody sees an opportunity to improve their station in life. Optimism abounds. Think back to that period following World War II. A booming economy buoyed a bold, optimistic view of the world: We can put a man on the Moon; we can build a Great Society, a racially integrated world. In our era, we can expect the same.

Also, in prosperous times, a spirit of generosity prevails. The vast majority of Americans who see their prospects rising with the expanding economy are genuinely sympathetic to the plight of those left behind. This kinder, gentler humanitarian urge is bolstered by a cold, hard fact: The bigger the network, the better. The more people in the network, the better for everyone. Wiring half a town is only marginally useful. If the entire town has phones, then the system really sings. Every person, every business, every organization directly benefits from a system in which you can pick up a phone and reach every individual rather than just a scattered few. That same principle holds true for the new networked computer technologies. It pays to get everyone tied into the new information grid. This mentality is becoming more and more pervasive. Almost everyone understands we're deep into the transition toward a networked economy and society. It makes sense to get everyone on board.

The welfare reform initiative of 1996 began the process of drawing the poor into the economy at large. At the time, political leaders weren't talking about the network effect so much as eliminating a wasteful government program. Nevertheless, the shakeup of the welfare system coincided with the growth of the economy. More and more welfare recipients have been getting jobs, and eventually many of them will move up to more skilled professions. This has helped to pare down the welfare rolls. What's more, former welfare recipients are not the only ones benefiting from the new economy; the working poor are getting more opportunities to leverage their way up to more stable lives.

As we get settled into a networked way of life, we will need to move on to a more ambitious global project: making a multicultural society really work. Though the United States has the mechanics—such as the legal framework—of an integrated society in place, Americans need to learn how to accept social integration on a deeper level. The underpinnings of a booming economy make efforts to ease the tensions among various ethnic and interest groups much easier than before because people are more tolerant of others when their own livelihoods are not threatened. But hopefully, people will also come to see diversity as a way to spark a creative edge. Part of the key to success in the future is to remain open to differences, to stay exposed to alternative ways of thinking. We need to recognize the wisdom of building a society that draws on the strengths and creativity of all people.

As the new century moves on, it will become clear to most people on the planet that if we want to continue to prosper, all cultures must coexist in relative harmony on a global scale. This, of course, will pave the way for a world religion and a world government.

9

The Religion of the Future

If there were one religion that could be said to best fit modern society's "whatever works for you is okay with me" mind-set, it would have to be New Age.

New Age "theology" represents a do-it-yourself form of religion. One can pick and choose whatever ideas, beliefs, concepts, and concerns happen to appeal to him personally. The rest can merely be set aside; they need not be rejected.

The bottom line is obvious. New Age theology rests upon pantheism, which is succinctly summarized in the following words:

> All is God,
> God is all,
> Man is part of it,
> Therefore, man is God.

According to New Age, the only thing separating man from God is his own consciousness, not his sin. Thus, New Agers propose finding God within oneself by altering one's consciousness through such means as meditation, chanting, channeling, sensory expansion, ecstatic dancing, and even fire walking. The New Age approach to spirituality is more a matter of experience than belief. An altered conscience is said to lead to self-realization, which then results in personal transformation (the New Ager's "salvation"). In this process, personal experience becomes the final authority for defining one's spiritual journey.

In his very helpful book *A Crash Course on the New Age Movement,* Elliot Miller defines the New Age movement as an informal network of individuals and organizations bound together by common values (mysticism and monism) and a common vision (the coming New Age of Aquarius).[1]

Within the New Age network are several separate strands that interconnect:

1. *Consciousness movement:* those advocating the expansion of human consciousness by altered mental states, resulting in the expansion of human awareness.

2. *Holistic health:* those encouraging better food and diet for better mental and spiritual development.

3. *Human potential:* the self-help psychology of self-awareness, self-actualization, and self-improvement.

4. *Eastern mysticism:* various gurus advocating transcendental meditation, astral projection, reincarnation, and various Hindu doctrines that view the material world as illusionary.

5. *Occultism:* pseudoscientific return to witchcraft, satanism, shamans, mediums, palm readers, and Tarot cards.

The blend of these elements varies with every individual and every subgroup within the New Age network. Some lean toward ecological issues (save the planet); others lean toward global peace issues (make love, not war); and still others prefer a mystical orientation that mixes meditation, yoga, ESP, and astrology with a strong belief in reincarnation. The combinations of any of these elements are like fingers of an intellectual hand reaching out to potential followers.

Miller states, "New Agers tend to be eclectic: they draw what they think is the best from many sources. Long-term exclusive devotion to a single teacher, teaching, or technique is not the norm. They move from one approach to another in their spiritual quests."[2] Thus, the subjective guides of experience and intuition are the final authorities for New Age thinkers. The Bible and the gospel message are vehemently rejected. Because there is no objective truth, the New Ager creates his or her own subjective truth. Therefore, the uniqueness of the gospel of salvation through Jesus Christ is quickly rejected with the statement, "That's your truth, but it's not for me."

Scientific Mysticism

Modern man has reached the point where he does not want to face the logical consequences of a secular world without God. But instead of repenting of his rebellion against God, he has now turned to a kind of scientific mysticism that has been popularized as the New Age movement.[3] Modern New Age mysticism is a combination of transcendentalism, spiritualism, Oriental mysticism, and transpersonal psychology. It rests upon the humanist psychology of Abraham Maslow, Fritz Perls, Carl Rogers, and Rollo May, all of whom emphasized the elevation of personal growth as the highest good and placed the transcendent at the top of the list of man's hierarchical needs.

The New Psychology, as it came to be called, developed a trend in therapy toward the deification of the isolated self and the rejection of traditional morality as moral blindness in favor of holistic psychic health. Thus, it developed hand in hand with the whole human potential movement. Key elements of New Age thought include restructuring the mind through meditation, sensory deprivation (for example, flotation therapy), and the self-tuning of the mind and body to become receptors and transmitters of cosmic forces. Psychic therapies claim to manipulate "life energies" to provide inner healing of individuals and to promote human relationships in harmony with cosmic forces.[4]

Author Dave Hunt is certainly correct in his observation that the whole of New Age mysticism is based upon Teilhard de Chardin's concept of the evolution of the soul.[5] Teilhard was a French Catholic priest, paleontologist, and theologian who attempted to "Christianize" evolution with a theistic view in which the soul emerged as the driving force of evolution. This evolution would lead to a collective superconsciousness of humanity, which in turn would result in a new age of life on earth.[6]

Teilhard's mysticism is expressed most clearly in his now popular Hymn of the Universe, in which he advocated the concept of centrism, or the tendency of things to converge and move to the center, resulting in the totalization of all phenomena.[7] This end result of spiritual evolution, he says, will be realized in a collectivism of all reality, by which everything will become a part of a new organic whole. Present human consciousness (noosphere) will culminate in a theosphere when converging human spirits transcend matter and space in a mystical union called the omega point.

It is this merging of scientific mysticism with a rejection of materialistic secularism that has resulted in New Age thinking. This thinking then couples with the human potential movement, which offers a number of techniques for advancing one's metaphysical evolution. Since all ideas have political consequences, we should not be surprised to discover that the political agenda of New Age thinking includes ecological concerns, sexual equality, and the unification of the world order by the transformation of the current political order through a "planetary consciousness."

The New Age transformationalists seek the total transformation of society along ideological lines consistent with their own beliefs. By challenging the "myths" of matter, time, space, and death, New Agers believe they will release our untapped human potential to create a new and better world.

The End of the Intellectual Rope

After looking for the solutions to the world's problems in education, science, technology, and other similar fields of endeavor, modern man has finally come to the conclusion that he needs hope beyond himself to solve those problems. He sees his choices as relatively few. He can turn to God, himself, others, nature, or a mystic collective consciousness. But in reality, he has only two choices: himself or God. Ironically, man's rationalism has driven him to irrationality. Either he must accept the logical consequences of living in a world without God or he must turn to God. All other options are merely wishful thinking.

While most people have chosen to turn away from God, they have found it difficult to throw God away altogether. They find consolation in the thought that someday, God or a higher power of some kind is going to come from outer space to save the world. Unfortunately, these people are looking for "salvation" in other kinds of supposed higher powers. Also unfortunate is that New Agers are unwilling to face the facts. There is no scientific proof for the mystical claims of reincarnation, spirit guides, astral projection, time travel, or a dozen other ideas popularized by New Age proponents. When the process of mystification is complete, it leaves man dangling at the end of his own intellectual rope—with nowhere to turn!

The spiritual void caused by the rejection of Christianity has left modern man desperately looking for a spiritual reality beyond himself. New Agers, however, argue that our overemphasis on rationality has caused us to lose our intuitive awareness. Like the old Jedi warrior in Star Wars, New Agers advise people to let their feelings guide them. The collective "force" of humanity (past and present) will guide you better than following mere objective facts.

In the end, objectivity is thrown out the window by New Agers, and they blame the rest of the world for its collective intellectual blindness. This has led to a great paradigm shift, or a new way of thinking about old problems. Leading the vanguard of New Age thinkers is Fritjof Capra, who argues that the old mechanistic perspective of the world must be replaced by the view that sees the world as one indivisible, dynamic whole whose parts are interrelated in the cosmic process.[8]

Following the earlier ideas of Austrian Ludwig von Bertalanffy and South African Jan Smuts, Capra promotes a holistic approach to solving social problems based upon the General Systems Theory (GST), which calls for the unification of the physical and social sciences to produce a great global society.

Selling It to the Public

In order to intellectually promote the idea of a New World Order, New Agers turn to mysticism as an ally to the systems movement. Synthesis replaces analysis of scientific data. The intuitive ability to recognize "wholes" replaces the need to analyze all the "parts." Capra states, "The systems view of life is spiritual in its deepest essence and thus consistent with many ideas held in mystical traditions."[9]

New Agers tie their concepts of an emerging world order to the concept of purposeful and creative evolution. Following the ideas of German philosopher G.W.F. Hegel, they view God as a process rather than a person. Thus, for New Agers, evolution is "God in process." Elliot Miller observes, "Without such faith in evolution, New Agers would be incapable of maintaining their distinctive optimism."[10]

Consequently, New Agers believe in the evolutionary emergence of a new collective consciousness that will result in a new humanity. They will solve the threats of nuclear war, ecological disaster, and economic collapse by an intuitive and mystical approach to life. New Age thinker Donald Keys put it like this: "A new kind of world—the world into which we are already moving—requires a new kind of person, a person with a planetary perspective."[11]

To make this hopeful human improvement work, New Agers propose a "quantum leap" forward in evolution. John White says, "We are witnessing the final phase of Homo sapiens and the simultaneous emergence of what I have named Homo Noeticus, a more advanced form of humanity....As we pass from the Age of Ego to the Age of God, civilization will be transformed from top to bottom. A society founded on love and wisdom will emerge."[12]

All of this may seem like intellectual wishful thinking in light of the human tragedies of crime, war, drought, and starvation. But to New Agers, it is a religion—with faith in evolution as the process and the worship of the planet as God. Teilhard himself, though a Jesuit Catholic paleontologist and philosopher, suggested that the planet earth was itself a living thing. Today it is called "Gaia" or "Terra," the mother-earth goddess of ancient mythology. It is further suggested that the mind of Gaia, in turn, must participate in some universal or cosmic mind. On this basis, New Agers call upon everyone to surrender their personal agendas to the ecological well-being of the living earth, Gaia. "Save the planet" is the evangelistic cry of the New Age movement.

A Return to Paganism

The New Age worship of the earth and the deification of the planet represent a return to primitive paganism. According to Margot Adler, a practicing witch and coven priestess, "the modern pagan resurgence includes the new feminist goddess worshiping groups, certain new religions based on the visions of science fiction writers, and attempts to revive the surviving tribal religions."[13] Judeo-Christian patriarchal religions with a Father-God figure are vehemently rejected in favor of goddess religions and witchcraft (or Wicca), which promote a spirituality of ecological wholeness and human pleasures.

While goddess religion has gained popularity because of its alignment with feminism, shamanism has exploded in popularity with men. Blending animism (spirit contact through natural objects; e.g., sacred trees or mountains) with pantheism (belief that all is God), shamans try to harmonize the natural and spiritual worlds. Following Native American tradition, shamans view themselves as spiritual masters rather than mere medicine men.

Shaman is a term adopted by anthropologists who studied the Tungus people of Siberia. It basically means "witch," "witch doctor," "medicine man," "sorcerer," "wizard," and so on. Shamanism is the most ancient system of mind-body healing known to humanity, and it represents the false religion that is under the influence of "the god of this world"—Satan!

Author Dave Hunt expresses a strong concern that modern shamanism is creeping into today's churches under the guise of psychological terms and labels.[14] The techniques of visualization, guided imagery, and inner healing have all been practiced in shamanism for thousands of years. But today they have been redefined as a part of the New Age language of transpersonal psychology. Some, like Morton Kelsey, have gone so far as to suggest that Jesus was the "greatest of all shamans."[15] Kelsey equates clairvoyance, telepathy, out-of-body experiences, ESP, and psychokinesis with manifestations of the power of God.

It is this kind of mental gymnastics that enables New Agers to redefine the terms and concepts of spirituality. They are ready to accept the earth or the self as God. They believe in extraterrestrial beings, angels, demons, witches, and wizards. Their influence can be seen in movies like *Star Wars, Ghost, Field of Dreams, E.T., Jewel of the Nile,* and *Dances with Wolves.* They see great spirituality in a diversity of role models, such as Native American medicine men, Hindu gurus, Tibetan lamas, Sufi mystics, Zen teachers, and Oriental hermits. But they are united in their rejection of God the Father, the deity of Christ, and the personality of the Holy Spirit.

The Counterfeit Christ

While New Age thinkers advocate Eastern mysticism, they often attempt to clothe it in Christian terminology. That's because those who grow up in Western society find Eastern spirituality and thought to be very different and foreign. Growing up in the Western world makes it difficult for some people to totally shed their religious heritage. So New

Agers repackage Eastern mysticism to make it more accept-
able to the Western mind. Douglas Groothuis of Probe
Ministries notes:

> New Age spirituality takes on a distinctive Western
> identity. Because the West still remembers its Chris-
> tian heritage, traffics in Christian images and
> bandies about Christian words, Christian symbols
> serve as a good medium for advancing the cause. The
> semantic rail system has already been laid by hun-
> dreds of years of Christian tradition, and the mes-
> sage is now steaming full speed ahead.[16]

New Agers have taken the Christ of the Bible and totally
reinterpreted and repackaged Him as the New Age Jesus.
New Agers separate the historical Jesus of Nazareth from
the Christ-consciousness that He came to attain. Jesus is not
the Way, the Truth, and the Life; He is a way-shower. He is
one of the Ascended Masters who realized oneness with
God, but He is not viewed as the unique and divine Son of
God. To New Agers, Christ is one of the monistic masters in
a whole pantheon of deities.

Actress Shirley MacLaine, a prominent New Age advocate, has said that Jesus "became an adept yogi and mastered
complete control over His body and the physical world
around Him....[He] tried to teach people that they would
do the same things if they got in touch with their spiritual
selves and their own potential power."[17]

New Agers like MacLaine leap to this conclusion by sug-
gesting that Jesus traveled to India during His silent years
before His public ministry. There He supposedly came
under the teachings of the Hindu masters—teachings that
He unsuccessfully attempted to communicate to the Jewish
community when He returned to Israel.

The counterfeit Christ of the New Age movement is being repackaged as a tolerant, broad-minded, nonjudgmental teacher. He is a way-shower who points men toward the god within themselves. As the cosmic Christ, He is now one of the Ascended Masters who continues to reveal Himself as an emissary of the kingdom of light.

In his very thorough study *The Counterfeit Christ of the New Age Movement*, Ron Rhodes of Reasoning with the Scriptures Ministries points out that New Agers have three ways of explaining away orthodox Christian beliefs:

1. They speak of supposed discoveries of hidden writings about Christ (e.g., Gnostic Gospels)

2. They promote new revelations of truth about Jesus from psychics and channelers

3. They speak of esoteric interpretations (deeper meanings) of Scripture.[18]

The details about Jesus may vary from one New Age teacher to the next.[19] David Spangler believed Jesus merely "attuned" to Christ and became His channel. Edgar Cayce taught that Jesus became the Christ in His thirtieth reincarnation. Levi Dowling believed Jesus became the Christ through ancient Egyptian initiation rites. Elizabeth Clare Prophet believes Jesus traveled to India as a child and eventually ascended to Christhood and returned to His homeland.

While the specific details may vary, all New Age thinkers agree that Christ is only one of many Ascended Masters who may serve as guides to the truth. New Age Christology is drawn from a vast array of existing religious and philosophical concepts that are eclectic and syncretistic to the extreme. In a do-it-yourself religion, one ought not be surprised to find a make-your-own Jesus!

Voices from the Dark Side

New Age thinking is rooted in the hippie counterculture of the 1960s and 1970s. Though the hippie movement died out after the Vietnam War, its ideas remained behind. Elliot Miller observes that New Agers are primarily baby-boomers (people born shortly after World War II) who have recycled, but not rejected, the ideals of the hippie counterculture: [20]

1. antimaterialism

2. utopianism

3. exaltation of nature

4. rejection of traditional morality

5. fascination with the occult

The New Age movement is not a passing fad. It has been gaining momentum for three decades and is still going strong. Yet most people didn't really notice the popular appeal of New Age thinking until the late 1980s. That's when actress Shirley MacLaine's autobiography *Out on a Limb* and several subsequent books openly promoted New Age ideals: "I am God," reincarnation, séances, crystals, and pyramid power. In August 1987, 20,000 New Agers gathered at various "sacred sites" around the world for the "Harmonic Convergence," a supposed cosmic event of great significance. By December 7, 1987, the New Age movement had made the cover of *Time* magazine.

Miller refers to the New Age subculture as "another America" existing alongside the secular and religious establishments and competing with them for cultural dominance.[21] He characterized New Agers as sincere, intelligent, optimistic, and humanitarian. Unlike traditional Eastern mystics, New Agers are positive about life and their involvement in the world. They embrace the future while promoting the ideals of global peace, economic prosperity, political unification, and ecological balance.

New Agers have been variously described as "Western mystics," "hippies come of age," "secular prosperity theologians," and "secularized spiritualists," but it is their combination of subjective spirituality and secular morality that leaves them so vulnerable to astrological and occultic influences.

The Age of Aquarius

New Agers hitchhike much of their ideology on the concepts of astrology, especially the idea of the "Age of Aquarius." New Agers believe that a spiritual age is now upon us in which many people are evolving into advanced stages of spiritual consciousness. They further believe that personal transformation must precede planetary transformation. This means that New Agers are committed to the proselytization of new "converts" to their cause. They are out to win over people to what some, like Marilyn Ferguson, have called "the Aquarian Conspiracy."[22]

Astrologers believe that human evolution is progressing in cycles corresponding to the signs of the Zodiac. Each cycle allegedly lasts about 2,000 years. Following the beliefs of astrologers, New Agers believe man is now moving from the Piscean (intellectual) Age into the Aquarian (spiritual) Age.

On April 25, 1982, millions of people in 20 major cities around the world were stunned by a large, full-page newspaper ad boldly proclaiming:

> THE WORLD HAS HAD ENOUGH—OF HUNGER, INJUSTICE, WAR. IN ANSWER TO OUR CALL FOR HELP, AS WORLD TEACHER FOR ALL HUMANITY. THE CHRIST IS NOW HERE.[23]

The advertisement went on to announce that since July 1977, the Christ has been "emerging as a spokesman" for the world community. "Throughout history," the ad continued, "humanity's evolution has been guided by a group of enlightened men, the masters of wisdom." The public notice went on to announce that the world teacher who stands at the center of this great spiritual hierarchy is Lord Maitreya, known to Christians as the Christ. Christians await the return of Christ, Jews await the coming of the Messiah, Buddhists look for the Fifth Buddha, Hindus expect the Lord Krishna, and Muslims await the Imam Mahdi. "These are all names for one individual," the ad proclaimed, assuring the readers of a New World Order of peace and prosperity.[24]

New Ager Benjamin Crème, an English esotericist who was a disciple of Theosophy's Helena Blavatsky and Alice Bailey, engineered the "Christ Is Now Here" ad campaign. Miller notes that if Blavatsky was the "grandmother" of the New Age movement, Alice Bailey would be its "mother."[25] She, more than any other individual, took the ideas of spiritualism and repackaged them into the basic tenets of the New Age movement. Crème, in turn, hit the road like an evangelist to promote these concepts on a nonstop, worldwide tour.

Constance Cumbey, a Christian attorney from Detroit, Michigan, first alerted the evangelical community in her book *The Hidden Dangers of the Rainbow*. While many feel she overreacted to the conspiracy threat from the New Age movement, no one can doubt her sincerity in attempting to alert the Christian public to what she discovered in New Age books, seminars, and lectures. Even Elliot Miller admits, "There is an 'Aquarian Conspiracy,' a conscious effort by a broad-based movement to subvert our cultural establishment so that we might enter a 'New Age' based on mysticism and occultism."[26]

New Age Activism

Since the publication of Mark Satin's *New Age Politics* in 1978, it has been clear that New Age activists intend to continue promoting a political agenda for a united global community under the control of a one-world government. New Agers are using the following means in order to convince society of the need for this new world order:

- *Psychic healing*—Using man's inner psychic energy to heal his emotional conflicts and distress.

- *Holistic health*—Combining diet and inner dynamic force to produce a healthy and productive life.

- *Transpersonal education*—Also called holistic education, it targets public education as the medium to combine humanistic and mystical approaches to learning.

- *Values clarification*—An educational technique that emphasizes that one's values emerge from within himself and not from external codes, such as the Ten Commandments.

- *Human Potential*—Thought-reform techniques promoting the use of guided imagery and visualization through organization development (O.D.) and organization transformation (O.T.) seminars. Used to bring humanistic psychology and Eastern mysticism into the workplace.

New Agers promote the basic human values of 1) survival, 2) interdependence, 3) autonomy, 4) humanness. This leaves little or no place for biblical Christianity. In fact, the occult connection found in New Age thinking is essentially anti-Christian. A new world order based upon New Age ideology would likely view evangelical Christianity as bigoted, divisive, and sectarian. This could easily set the stage for the justified persecution of Christians as rebels against the Aquarian regime. Elliot Miller warns, "Christian dogmatism could easily be viewed (in fact, already is) as anti-revolutionary—a threat to the global unity necessary for racial survival. And when survival dominates over all other values, the elimination of any perceived threat to it could easily be 'justified.'"[27]

New Age Spiritism

The gasoline that drives the New Age engine is spiritism, which is the practice of communicating with departed human spirits or extrahuman intelligences through a human medium by the process of channeling. In his recent book *Channeling*, Jon Klimo claims that channeling involves a human being who is possessed by an external force, power, or personality.[28] This entity exercises control over the perceptual, cognitive, and self-reflective capacities of the person, who has relinquished himself to the external force.

The Bible clearly warns against involvement with witchcraft, séances, and mediums. Deuteronomy 18:10-12 commands, "Let no one be found among you...who is a medium or a spiritist or who consults the dead. Anyone who does these things is detestable to the LORD." The prophet Isaiah warned, "When men tell you to consult mediums and spiritists, who whisper and mutter, should not a people inquire of their God? Why consult the dead on behalf of the living?" (8:19-20).

Scripture acknowledges the reality of demonic spirits and their attempts to communicate through human mediums (see 1 Samuel 28:6-14; Acts 16:16-19). It always presents them as evil, deceptive, and malevolent. They are channels to Satan's lies, not to God's truth.

The Ultimate Seduction

Elliot Miller observes that the varied messages of the channels are ultimately the same: We are gods; we don't need a savior other than ourselves; there is no sin or death; we create our own reality. New Agers imply there is no objective truth, only subjective "truth." Since we create our own truth, we create our own reality. Miller writes, "Once the New Ager accepts this premise, an almost insurmountable barrier to Christian penetration is erected."[29] No matter what appeal the Christian makes, the New Agers will tend to dismiss it as irrelevant to his own personal "reality."

Desperately seeking answers to the great human problems of inner spirituality, personal growth, true peace, and security, the New Ager turns to himself, the planet, the forces of nature, and the spirit world for help. In all this quest, he misses the true Christ, the real source of the peace, security, and stability he seeks.

In the meantime, New Agers are left hoping for a great cosmic deliverer to come rescue the world and preserve its peace. Constance Cumbey is right when she says, "For the first time in history there is a viable movement—the New Age movement—that truly meets all the scriptural requirements for the antichrist and the political movement that will bring him on the world scene."[30]

The stage has certainly been set for a new world order based upon a subjective view of reality. It will only be a matter of time, then, before the objective standards of truth will have totally eroded in the modern world. We are getting closer to the end. The only real question left is this: How much time do we still have before it's too late?

10

Globalism and the World Economy

Our world is moving rapidly toward a global economy. This is happening on several fronts: One, world leaders are pressing hard to lessen economic disparities and differences between countries; and two, they are lowering or even doing away with trade barriers. What's more, the Internet has made all sorts of goods much more readily accessible all over the world. And these are just some of the foundational steps toward a global economy; there's much more we have not touched upon. And according to Bible prophecy, it will all culminate into a one-world government economy headed up by the Antichrist: "No one could buy or sell unless he had the mark, which is the name of the beast or the number of his name" (Revelation 13:17).

Robert Reich of Harvard University recently stated: "We are living through a transformation that will rearrange the politics and economics of the coming century....Each nation's primary political task will be to cope with the centrifugal forces of the global economy."[1] Reich sees the coming global economy as an inevitable force that will virtually sweep nationalism away. The value of a given society or an individual worker will be his or its ability to contribute to the world economy.

From Local to National to Global

During the nineteenth century, closely knit networks of local economies were transformed into national economies. Today the national economies are being transformed into a global one. Initially, America led the way toward a global economy modeled on American capitalism. Today the new Europe is leading the way to a system that is often viewed as capable of setting the economic standards for the whole world.

Such ideas as "buy America" are becoming less of a reality all the time. Reich notes that when an American buys a Pontiac from General Motors, he or she engages unwittingly in an international transaction. "Of $20,000 paid to GM, approximately $5,600 goes to South Korea for routine labor; $3,500 goes to Japan for advanced components; $1,500 to West Germany for styling and design engineering; $800 to Taiwan, Singapore, and Japan for small electronic components; $500 to Britain for advertising and marketing services; and about $100 to Ireland and Barbados for data processing. The balance of $8,000 goes to manufacturers in Detroit, bankers and lawyers in Washington, and General Motor's stockholders."[2]

This is a typical example of how the "global web" already works. In time, this web will become even more complex, touching virtually every industry in America. The interrelations of multinational corporations and the international cooperation of corporations within different nations are not only the trend of the future: it is here now.

Caught in the Global Web

Gilbert Williamson, president of NCR Corporation, recently said, "We at NCR think of ourselves as a globally competitive company that happens to be headquartered in the United States."[3] Like many American products, many American corporations are becoming more and more internationalized. They are fast becoming part of the global web in which much of what they buy and sell comes from other countries.

For example, 40 percent of IBM's world employees are non-Americans. Robert Reich notes that IBM Japan employs 18,000 Japanese workers, and with annual sales of $6 billion, it is one of Japan's leading exporters of computers.[4] The question is this: Is IBM Japan an American or Japanese company...or both?

Whirlpool is in an even more complex situation. It recently cut its American work force by 10 percent, shifted production to Mexico, bought Dutch-owned Phillips appliances, and now employs 43,500 people in 45 countries. Is it an American company because it has an American headquarters or because the majority of its stockholders are Americans? Or is it an international company that happens to be headquartered in America?

Who Will Lead the Way?

No country is better positioned to lead the way in the economic boom of the twenty-first century than the United States. John Naisbitt writes:

> In the global economic competition of the information economy, the quality and innovativeness of human resources will spell the difference. In this regard no country in the world is better positioned than the United States.[5]

Naisbitt and Pat Aburdene go on to predict that well-educated, skilled information workers will earn the highest wages in history, further reinforcing an economic boom in the years ahead. They argue that the further the information economy evolves, the better the economy will do in the future as the middle class moves upward in its mobility.

In the meantime, the European Union is trying to catch up to the United States and Japan. Naisbitt and Aburdene note that the changes in Europe are economically driven as a response to the global competition. "Politics is not driving the change," they observe, "but is being pulled by it."[6]

The philosophy behind the New Europe is to forge one cohesive market that can compete on a global scale. In order for this to become a reality, physical barriers, such as customs posts and border controls, will have to be removed. Technical barriers involving different standards and regulations will have to be unified. And fiscal barriers, such as taxes, will have to be standardized. When the process is complete, it will mean:

- A Greek lawyer could set up a practice in Barcelona, and a Spanish shoe company could open a shop in Ireland.

- American businesspeople will be able to fly to Europe, pass through customs once, and visit 11 different member countries.

- A British bank could be a partner in the Paris fashion industry.

All in all, these developments would bring about more competition at all levels of the single market, bringing a greater choice of goods and services at better prices. For most Europeans this will be a tremendous step forward economically. And, the presence of a high-speed computer network across Europe will bring the continent together in a manner that no military or political action could ever hope to do. Thus, the political unification of Europe will ride on the shoulders of the economy.

11

The Struggle for World Dominion

We have now moved to the final round in the struggle for world dominion. The collapse of communism has removed one of the significant players in what one writer has called the "great millennial endgame."[1] But the end of the Cold War is by no means the end of the struggle for world supremacy. As we approach the third millennium of church history, the immanency of a one-world government seems closer than ever.

Everyone realizes that we are standing on the edge of a new day in world politics. The dramatic changes we have witnessed in Europe, the Middle East, and the former Soviet Union tell us that the world is undergoing a massive transformation. The aftermath of World War II finally has been shaken from us like an old rag. Eastern Europe is awakening to a new day of hope and freedom.

At the same time, there is great concern about where all these changes are taking us. Charles Colson recently said, "We sense that things are winding down, that somehow freedom, justice, and order are slipping away. Our great

175

civilization may not yet lie in smoldering ruins, but the enemy is within the gates. The times seem to smell of sunset."[2] He went on to suggest that Western civilization is facing the greatest crisis encountered since the barbarians invaded Rome.

Robert Hughes, in a recent essay entitled "The Fraying of America," observes that we are a society "obsessed with therapies and filled with distrust…skeptical of authority and prey to superstition."[3] He reminds us it was just over 50 years ago that W.H. Auden foresaw our day through the eyes of Herod in *For the Time Being* (London: Faber & Faber, 1944). In this fascinating portrayal, Herod muses over the unpleasant task of slaughtering the innocent children at Bethlehem in order to eliminate Christ. Herod rationalized that if he allowed the Christ child to escape, "reason will be replaced by revelation. Objective rational law will be replaced by subjective visions…of a New Age."[4]

Reason Above Revelation

Ironically, that is exactly where life went in the 1990s. Our neglect of God's revelation has pushed us to the limits of our own rationalization. We have abandoned rationality for irrationality in the attempt to hold onto belief in something—anything—beyond ourselves.

All through the twentieth century, we allowed godless secularism to replace the Judeo-Christian values of our society. God was deliberately and systematically removed from prominence in our culture and in our intellectual lives. We have made Him irrelevant to our culture. Tragically, we have also made our culture irrelevant to God. In so doing, we have abandoned our spiritual heritage. The Christian consensus that once dominated Western culture is now shattered. The world is already mired in the quicksand of secularism, relativism, and mysticism. It is a wonder we have survived as long as we have.

We should not be surprised, then, that spiritual confusion is rampant. Almost daily someone launches a new religion, predicts the end of the world, or announces himself to be the Messiah. Is it any wonder that a nonbelieving world shakes its head and walks away?

In the place of biblical Christianity, people are now calling for a new world order that consists of the very elements Scripture warns will signify the empire of the Antichrist:

1. *World Government*—Globalists are now insisting that national governments should surrender their sovereignty to a one-world government. Such a government would operate through a world headquarter, a world court, and even a world military.

2. *World Economy*—This aspect of globalism is already upon us. No developed nation of any kind can survive today without networking with the global economy. There is almost no such thing as an "American" product that is not dependent on parts, trade, or investments from foreign countries.

3. *World Religion*—This will be the final phase of the new world order. The idea of a new world religion of peace and cooperation is already being proposed. Pope John Paul II, the Dalai Lama, and leaders of the World Council of Churches have endorsed religious unity.

What we are witnessing today may well be the fulfillment of the biblical prophecies of the end times. Prophecy expert Peter Lalonde sees a parallel between the predictions in Revelation 13 and the current move toward a new world order.[5] Revelation 13 predicts the rise of a powerful world ruler who is able to control the world politically and economically. This ruler will have at his side a false prophet who promotes a one-world religion.

Lalonde writes, "It is breathtaking to realize that what we are witnessing today in the emergence of the 'New World Order' may well be a fulfillment of Revelation 13! In the world's rejection of the true Prince of Peace and in their rush to build their own earthly kingdom, the Antichrist's government is being fabricated for him!"[6]

A New World Order

Former President Bush observed, "A new partnership of nations has begun, and we stand today at a unique and extraordinary moment...out of these troubled times...a new world order can emerge."[7] When George Bush met with former Soviet leader Mikhail Gorbachev on the island of Malta in 1989, *Time* magazine flashed the startling headline: "Building a New World Order."[8] In his historic meeting with Pope John II, Gorbachev admitted to "having embarked upon the road of radical reform...[and] crossing the line beyond which there is no return to the past."[9]

Former Jesuit scholar Malachi Martin has suggested that the struggle for the new world order will come down to three major powers: Western capitalists, Eastern socialists, and the Catholic church. Martin observes, "There is one great similarity shared by all three of these geopolitical competitors. Each one has in mind a particular grand design for one-world governance."[10] Martin theorizes that just as the Soviet Union lost its hegemony in Eastern Europe, so also will the United States lose its hegemony in world politics. Then—and only then, Martin suggests—will the Pope make his move toward world dominion.

The Fall of Communism

Undoubtedly, the most dramatic event of our lifetime has been the sudden and apparent collapse of the Soviet Union. Mikhail Gorbachev's policy of *glasnost* ("openness") toward democracy brought down the Berlin Wall and the Iron Curtain in one fell swoop. The former Soviet leader's willingness to release the East-European satellite countries did not protect a reformed communism within the Soviet Union; rather, it opened the floodgates for cries of freedom within the Soviet Union as well.

By Christmas Day of 1989, communism lay dead in the streets of Eastern Europe. Germany was talking reunification; East and West Berliners were dancing in the streets; Poland was getting ready to elect Lech Walesa as president; and Romania's Nicolae Ceausescu, the last of the communist dictators, was executed in Bucharest. In a startlingly short amount of time, Eastern Europe was free at last!

This was Gorbachev's great gamble in the "great millennial endgame." By letting the satellites go, he hoped to communicate that he was concentrating on improving the Soviet economy at home, but alas, the strategy failed. The smell of freedom was being blown by the winds of change all the way to Moscow.

The Soviet citizens wanted more—much more! They, too, wanted to be rid of the dreaded system that had enslaved them for nearly 75 years. Public demonstrations began to mount against the government. Soon, upstart Boris Yeltsin was elected president of Russia and Gorbachev was forced to share the political spotlight with him. Then came the foiled coup attempt in August 1991. The Communist party hard-liners made one last desperate attempt to hold onto their power by kidnapping the Soviet leader. But huge crowds of people jammed Red Square and shouted allegiance to Yeltsin.

The military backed down. The coup failed because of a lack of popular support from the people. Ironically, the very movement that began as a people's revolution ended the same way. The people themselves stood up and demanded democracy and freedom, and to the surprise of the whole world, the people won! The "Evil Empire," with all its KGB agents, sinister intentions, nuclear weapons, and military might fell in one week to the people themselves.

Communism had impoverished every facet of individual life—spiritual values, human rights, social programs, and the economy. People had simply had enough and said so! Their spontaneous grassroots revolt was like a gale-force wind hurtling across Eastern Europe, knocking down every obstacle to democracy.

The New Europe

Today there is a new wave of optimism sweeping across Europe. By the end of 1992, the economic unification of the European Community became complete. "We are past the point of no return," announced Jacques Delors, the father of European unification.[11] The Europe of the future may well become a political union, the United States of Europe. If this happens, Europe, not America, could end up becoming the strongest and most powerful "nation" on earth—economically, politically, and even militarily. And if the current European Community were to continue to expand into the former Soviet satellites of Eastern Europe and even into Russia itself, Europe would stretch from the Atlantic Ocean to the Pacific Ocean for the first time in history!

The key players in the New Europe are England, Germany, and Russia. The unification or cooperation of these three superstates could well determine the issue of who controls the world of the future. Already Chancellor Helmut Kohl of the reunified Germany is calling for Germany to "take a bigger role...in the community of nations."[12]

As Germany struggles to reassert her leadership on the Continent, at least one writer has observed, "With the collapse of the Soviet Union and its empire, the logic behind Germany's subordinate role...has also collapsed, and the postwar balance of power on the European continent has been upset."[13] What role Germany will play in the future remains to be seen. Some see her taking a passive role in international politics; others fear the rise of the "Fourth Reich."

The new Soviet Union, the Commonwealth of Independent States, could also emerge as a major player in European politics. It is still too early to tell how the new order of this part of the world will shape up or if Russia's current government will even persevere. While the label "Soviet Union" may be gone, the reality still remains. The vast land of 250 million people with hundreds of thousands of nuclear weapons still exists.

Many Christians believe that the resurgence of the New Europe fulfills the biblical prophecies of a revived Roman Empire in the last days. Like the architects of the Tower of Babel, advocates of the new world order believe that "coming together" will consolidate what were formerly volatile or weak economies and foster global peace and cooperation. Helmut Kohl has said, "The United States of Europe will form the core of a peaceful order...the age prophesied of old, when all shall dwell secure and none shall make them afraid."[14]

The real tragedy in all this talk of global unity is the absence of any emphasis on the spiritual roots of democracy and freedom. The gospel has been blunted in Western

Europe for so long that there is little God-consciousness left in the European people. Without Christ, the Prince of Peace, there can be no hope for manmade orders of peace and prosperity. There will be no millennium without the Messiah!

In the present configuration of nations, the Islamic world seems out of step with all the talk of a new world order. It seems to have only one agenda: an Islamic World Order. There is little or no room in Islam for pluralism on religious or political issues. Muslims believe they are right and all others, including Christians and Jews, are infidels.

Where Are We Now?

What is now clearer than ever is that we have taken a quantum leap toward the fulfillment of the biblical prophecies of the last days. The stage is now being set for the final climatic act in the long history of the human drama. Things could not have been arranged more perfectly to set the stage for the fulfillment of the prophecies of the end times:

1. The fall of communism has paved the way for a world economy and a world government. The global web is tightening around us every day.

2. Secularism is giving way to New Age mysticism as the do-it-yourself religion of our times. The end result will be the watering down of religious beliefs so that they are more palatable to the general public.

3. Global economic interdependence will eventually lead to a global political system that dominates national sovereignty.

4. Materialism and selfism are replacing spiritual values. Mankind will be left in the mindless pursuit

of material prosperity as the basis for meaning and value in life.

5. The spiritual vacuum that results will leave the world ready for the ultimate deception: the Great Lie of the Antichrist that will deceive the whole world.

6. A world leader will quickly arise on the international scene promising to bring peace and economic stability. He will receive the support of the European community and eventually control the whole world.

7. A crisis in the Middle East will trigger this world leader's intervention militarily and politically. Eventually he will sign a peace treaty with Israel, only to break it later.

8. A false prophet of international fame will suddenly emerge to gain control of the world religious system and use it to reinforce the worship of Antichrist.

9. All resistance to the world system will be crushed by massive worldwide persecution. Men, women, and children will be slaughtered in the name of the world state.

10. Israel will become the central figure in the conflict with the world state. The Antichrist will eventually break his covenant with Israel and invade her land, setting the stage for the Battle of Armageddon.

How Close Are We to the End?

There is no doubt that we are fast approaching the final chapter of human history. The hoofbeats of the four horsemen of the Apocalypse can now be heard in the distance. The stage is set for the final act of the human drama.

The clock is ticking away the last seconds of any hope for a reprieve. We are being swept down the corridor of time to an inevitable date with destiny.

How much time is left? Only God knows. Thus we must use every means at our disposal to preach the gospel of God's saving grace everywhere we can while there is still time. This is not the time to rest on our laurels. Rather, we have a window of opportunity, by the grace of God, and we need to take advantage of it right now. It is time for us Western Christians to take seriously our responsibility to evangelize the world in our lifetime.

For over 75 years, Christians prayed for a spiritual breakthrough in the Iron Curtain. That time came. And since then, many other doors have opened. We must respond by mobilizing workers, financial resources, printed materials, and broadcasting equipment to get the gospel into the places where the gospel was prohibited for so long.

Jesus Christ said what we all must realize at this crucial hour: "As long as it is day, we must do the work of him who sent me. Night is coming, when no one can work" (John 9:4). To the ancient church at Philadelphia, our Lord said, "I have placed before you an open door that no one can shut" (Revelation 3:8). May we make the most of the opportunity we have right now, recognizing that the ultimate struggle for world dominion is between the forces of Christ and the forces of Satan.

12

The Coming Tribulation

There is really no beginning to the time when Satan started his fight to rule the world, unless you want to go all the way back to the battles in heaven and the temptation at the Garden of Eden. For ages since, he has wormed his way around, looking for weaknesses and filling every unwitting soul with his own evil cravings. Through his followers, he and his army reigned supreme. And the world will become much worse during the Tribulation, when the influence of the Holy Spirit and the Christian church is gone.

Imagine what it will be like in a world without God, absolutely void of goodness. Here's how the apostle Paul describes it:

> The secret power of lawlessness is already at work; but the one who now holds it back will continue to do so till he is taken out of the way. And then the lawless one will be revealed, whom the Lord Jesus will overthrow with the breath of his mouth and destroy by the splendor of his coming. The coming of the lawless one will be in accordance with the

work of Satan displayed in all kinds of counterfeit miracles, signs and wonders, and in every sort of evil that deceives those who are perishing. They perish because they refused to love the truth and so be saved. For this reason God sends them a powerful delusion so that they will believe the lie and so that all will be condemned who have not believed the truth but have delighted in wickedness (2 Thessalonians 2:7-12).

Future Story: The Root of All Evil

The powerful delusion overcame Gerald Litman as it did many others. In the early twenty-first century, Gerald was a very successful entrepreneur. He was the president of TrafficAir, the multibillion dollar website distributor of personal communications devices. They were headquartered in Los Angeles, California. The company sold anything and everything that had to do with personal airwave communications.

TrafficAir started out with cellular phones and notebook computers in the late 1990s and made a name for themselves. Then, shortly after the year 2000, things really took off! Cellular phone lines became faster, and computer hardware grew smaller and more powerful. More and more people worldwide were becoming a part of the Internet and making use of wireless communications devices. In a few more years the company sold its first TrafficAir Lifebook, a small handheld computer that had all of the features of a large notebook computer but used the lenses instead of a computer screen. These lenses functioned as a computer screen, or as a virtual-reality viewer. The lenses also had a small microphone built into their frame that would accept voice commands from the user.

In another year, the technology improved to the point where the whole LifeBook could be clipped onto one's belt but had the computing power and memory-storage capacity of a full-sized system. Also, TrafficAir was able to build the LifeBooks so they were true only to their owner, recognizing only the authorized user's retina and voice impressions so that misappropriation was not a worthwhile endeavor for the criminally minded.

Soon the LifeBooks were able to communicate at still higher speeds and people started to enjoy life like never before. They were banking, buying and selling stocks, getting information on the Internet, bidding at auctions, enjoying movies and music videos, and even participating in meetings and conferences all from the privacy and comfort of their very own space.

A Prophetic TV Commercial

You might have seen a commercial on television where an English-speaking man is in a park in Europe trading American stocks. He is looking at the stock quotes on the lenses of his eyeglasses and speaking his orders into a microphone that is part of the same headgear. In a moment, he becomes more animated and starts to shout, "Sell, sell!" His yelling and flailing arms even scares away the pigeons around him.

Then he quiets down and it is evident that a call came into his headgear, as he seems to be talking to a friend or family member back in the United States. He says he will be leaving on the afternoon flight. The impression given is that he is a businessman who was in Europe conducting business and that he took a few minutes to check his stocks. Finally, he's headed home.

It's interesting to note that the various elements of this prophetic television commercial are already reality in today's world. We already have an Internet that is talking to us. We already have various wireless devices that give us stock quotations through thin air. We already have virtual-reality eyeglasses that can show us whatever a computer screen can already show us. And we already have computers that can be trained to accept our voice commands!

What actually occurs in the commercial is this: The man's voice commands are turned into digital commands that are sent to the nearest broadcast (cellular) tower in Europe. His digital commands are then broadcast to the stateside trading firm with which he is registered, authorizing his transaction to take place. Moments later, he receives both an audio and visual response confirming the transaction is complete. Now, extend those capabilities to include a myriad of other tasks on earth!

How would you like to receive your daily mail electronically from anywhere in the world? Upon checking your mail, you would see a list. You would "open" the items you wanted to read or review, and save those that you didn't have time to deal with at the moment. You could verbally pay your bills immediately, and save the personal greetings for later. You could update your calendar with any new information that came in your mail. And you could delete the junk mail without paying the refuse industry a penny!

How would you like to watch the latest theater releases in three dimensions? How would you like to *participate* in the movie and see what effect your input has on the outcome of the movie? How would you like to do all of that with the same headset you use to check your mail? Perhaps while you are sitting in your easy chair, or while you are moving about in a virtual world?

How would you like to attend a meeting or conference without leaving your house? How would you like going to church and having an interactive Sunday school class with all your friends from all over the world—right in your own living room? How would you like to attend a concert without fighting the traffic and parking? The possibilities for entertainment and personal satisfaction are almost endless, but they can also be destructive.

One Man's Downfall

It was in 2005 that Gerald Litman took advantage of this headgear technology and started a company that made him lots of money, LoveVisor. This company sold virtual sex to lonely people. Frankly, there was more money to be made selling sex than anything else. People were willing to pay the price, whatever it was, to make them happy and feed their self-serving natures. The products and services were carefully tailored to promote every depraved concept possible as long as a dollar could be made. The human condition made it possible; LoveVisor was able to give them a realistic feeling of sexual excitement without all of the cumbersome issues associated with a relationship.

Litman, needless to say, wasn't a believer in Jesus Christ, except to admit that Christ was a good Jewish boy who did a fine job showing us how to live. He thought the Bible was comprised of fairy tales written by self-righteous men from 2,000 years ago. Adding to his contempt of Christians were his memories of the evangelists on television who had a money-hungry approach to preaching.

Computers, communications, and technology in general continued to move forward exponentially year after year. With the fortune Gerald made with the LoveVisor, he imagineered (used his imagination to create a new product) the company toward the new future…a bold place where people would be free of all encumbrances and be able to enjoy their lives to the utmost. He worked on a concept for two years and finally devised what he knew would be the most incredible product of all time—the LifeLine.

LifeLine Technology

Private enterprise is making major progress in microchip implants. Earlier we introduced you to Applied Digital Solutions, ranked as one of the fastest-growing technology companies in the country. If you haven't already, go to their website at www.adsx.com. You will find they are a company that specializes in e-commerce and retail business solutions.

Recently, Applied Digital Solutions purchased a company that specializes in implanting microchips in animals. Here's what is involved in this form of technology:

> The smallest microchip is about the size of a grain of rice. All Destron Fearing microchips are individually inscribed and programmed to store a unique,

permanent, 10- to 15-digit alphanumeric identification code. The microchip is coupled with an antenna and sealed in an inert glass capsule. The microchip is implanted into an animal using a procedure similar to a routine vaccination. After implantation, the device remains with the animal for life, where it provides the animal's unique ID number anytime it is scanned by a compatible electronic ID scanner. Once implanted into the animal, the microchip remains inactive until read with a scanner that sends a low-frequency radio signal to the chip, providing the power needed by the microchip to send its unique code back to the scanner and positively identify the animal. The use of a Destron microchip allows the ID number to be stored permanently inside the animal, just under the skin, where it cannot be lost or altered. The microchip will last for the life of the animal with the unique ID number intact.[1]

We also previously mentioned a similar product for humans, called Digital Angel, which can help to find humans who need to be located quickly. Most of us would agree that this Digital Angel could indeed be considered an angel when it is used to save a life, capture an escaped convict, or stop a terrorist plan in its tracks. However, we would also have to consider that with such a device we would lose control of our privacy and freedom.

What's more, this technology is disturbing because it can be used to identify specific people who have permission to buy and sell, as described in Revelation 13:16-17, which tells us about the mark of the beast. Taking a proper Christian perspective on this matter, we do not think that any specific company is in any way part of a conspiracy to implement a tribulation-era technology. What we believe is that the technology will become available, but we do not know who will use it for wrongful purposes or when.

Future Story: His Greed Turns to Misery

A person on the LifeLine was tuned into the entire world all at once. It was an exploration of knowledge, entertainment, and physical sensations all at the same time. The technology for LifeLine grew out of the virtual-reality sensations that became so popular with the LoveVisor accompanied by the technologies used in cloning and DNA research, but it was much more than any one of those. It was just what the name implies: a line to life. It became so popular so quickly that it exceeded all of the expectations of Gerald Litman and his associates. He became a billionaire shortly after it hit the market.

Gerald had everything in life that he had ever wanted and yet he was unhappy. He had his beautiful wife, Ruth (who professed to be a Christian), and their son and daughter, who were in their early elementary-school years. Everything seemed perfect. But even with his ideal life in his ideal house in his ideal neighborhood, Gerald Litman was emotionally distraught. He was not content with his lot in life. The world was his oyster and yet the oyster was not perfect. His own riches weren't enough. He wanted the world to be a better place. He thought he was being altruistic when he questioned the value of his personal riches if the world didn't offer him an equally perfect place to enjoy. Indeed, the world had become a worse place to live in many respects, even though wonderful innovations made many aspects of life better every day.

For example, science could not only clone animals, but also humans and body parts. Advancement in medicine and health helped to extend the expected lifespan of human beings by another 40 years. People were now smarter and healthier than ever. Many of the ailments of the twentieth century were gone. And yet the world was still suffering and getting worse. Divorces had climbed to new highs. Children no longer respected life. Drugs, gambling, and prostitution had all been decriminalized. Even though AIDS, cancer, and many deadly diseases had been cured, there were new and exotic ailments taking their toll upon society. Small countries battled and floundered and fell to revolutions and coups. Some suspected that biological warfare was being used to commit genocide on unsuspecting third world countries. There were more natural catastrophes than ever, too—earthquakes, volcanoes, and floods. It seemed like Mother Nature was rebelling, and the entire world, despite the fact everyone was now interconnected through communications networks and the new economy, was becoming a place full of peoples and countries paranoid of one another. Self-protection was becoming more and more the rule of the day.

Then came the most difficult catastrophe of all. Gerald had just gotten into his car to drive home from work late one night when he turned on the radio and heard that all the police stations throughout the Los Angeles area were getting an incredibly high number of missing persons reports. Also unusual was that many abandoned vehicles were littering the roads. Even the police and fire departments were missing workers, and stories were starting to come in from all over the country reporting the instantaneous disappearances of people. Gerald stopped the car even before it was out of the parking lot and called home. No answer. He drove home quickly, past the abandoned cars he had heard about, which included police cars, taxis, delivery trucks, semi trucks, and more. He rushed home in an absolute panic. It was a very eerie ride, as many people who were equally panicked were rushing about, uncertain of what was going on.

When Gerald arrived home, nobody was there. The beds had been slept in, but were now empty. The alarm had been set and didn't show it had been disengaged or set off. He couldn't see any evidence that anyone had left the house. What could have happened? Gerald called everyone he knew, and most of them were okay, but many of them knew one or more people who had disappeared in a similar fashion. Nobody had any answers. Gerald was crushed and confused.

You know what happened, of course—the rapture. But it would be quite some time before Gerald Litman learned the truth. The newspapers and media cited expert after expert for the next several weeks, all of whom reported the facts about the losses but offered little help as to why the losses had occurred. The losses had happened worldwide, and one interesting observation was that Israel had suffered serious losses, but the Islamic nations had not. In the meantime, tensions ran high between nations and between peoples.

The United Nations began an investigative commission. Their experts, supposedly the best the world had to offer, issued its final report eighteen months later. There was absolutely no direct evidence to support their findings since there were no bodies on which to conduct autopsies, but their conclusion seemed logical: An unknown terrorist group had somehow implemented a plan to inflict catastrophic damage on the earth—there were many groups known to have the willingness, including some headquartered within Muslim nations. By now, the western world was referring to this holocaust as the Great Atrocity. The experts did not point a finger at any one country or group in their report, but Israel, the United States, and most of Europe blamed Muslim terrorists.

The hard-core scientific community had a different perspective on the losses. They hypothesized that those who disappeared must have possessed a gene that made them susceptible to a biological agent that had been used in mass quantities. They had several different theories as to the biological agent that was used. They made up some agents and tested them on animals and found they could produce the same results—within moments, the animals were made to disappear without a trace. Most scientists agreed that, because the losses happened simultaneously all over the world, the biological agent had somehow been placed in the water supplies of many nations (perhaps through cloud seeding?). They theorized that the biological agent then adapted itself to certain gene pools and awaited a radio signal that would set them off. It took the brightest scientists in the world almost two years to arrive at this conclusion and duplicate the results on animals in the laboratory, and it was the only explanation that made sense from a scientific viewpoint.

Not everyone accepted the terrorist or biological agent answers. But to some, the answers were plausible. They knew that Muslim terrorism was at an all-time high. They also knew that Israel had long refused to give up the Temple Mount in Jerusalem to the Muslims. The religious rhetoric

and saber rattling between the Israelis and Muslims may
have finally led some radical terrorists to resort to drastic
measures.

In the Future At the Temple

"One of the most exciting events of recent months has
been the news that water is flowing from the holy rock of
Abraham and Isaac, on the Temple Mount. We now know
that water is definitely flowing from under the rock. The
Arabs on the Temple Mount deny this, while unsuccessfully trying to stop the flow. They have brought in special
pumps for this purpose, but the water continues. Nothing
can stop it.

"Our people have checked this and even photographed it.
With the help of hundreds of workers from the Islamic
movement, the Arabs are busy with intensive excavations
on the Temple Mount. The purpose of these is to destroy
the last remains of the First and Second Temples, so they
can deny the Jewish identity of the Temple Mount.
According to one account, during these diggings they
broke into one of the water sources, and the water started
to flow out from the rock. They temporarily diverted the
water in another direction, unknown to us. This news was
spread all over Israel and gave joy and hope to Israelis
looking for a sign of the redemption."

Another report about the water flowing from the Temple
Mount comes from the Israeli newspaper, *HaTsofer*. In the

May 15 edition of the journal, page 5, Eliazer Shaffer states that an Arab neighbor, Mohammed, shared with him in secret and with emotion, about this flow of water. He said that he had not seen it himself, but that he had heard that the Islamic Mufti of Jerusalem were very concerned by the flow because, according to Islamic writings, this was a good sign for the Jews, but a bad one for the Muslims. The people we sent to check the situation could not see the water, but learned that the Arabs on the Temple Mount have done everything possible to stop the flow of water, including using special pumps that they brought in for that purpose.[2]

Indeed, tensions are high in the Middle East today, and war could easily break out for a number of reasons—What shall be the reason for the war between the Jews and the Arabs? Will it be religious fervor, water supply necessary for Israel's survival, the oil owned by the Arab nations, the politics of the ownership of Jerusalem and the Temple Mount, or perhaps even an accident of some kind?

Future Story: Gog and Magog

As the world struggled to cope with the loss caused by the Great Atrocity, the relations between the Arab nations and the rest of the world were strained at best. The public concern was enormous. What gene would be susceptible next? When would another atrocity hit? Pressure was placed on various world governments to react with force. There was even talk of retaliation by the United Nations. Because no specific group or country could be blamed, no actions were taken. The Great Atrocity would go on to be remembered by the world, which voiced, with resolve, the sentiments following the Jewish Holocaust: "Never again."

One day a young Muslim boy walked into a Jewish synagogue in Jerusalem and sat behind a family that attended on every Sabbath. This boy had a small bag with him. Inside were crayons, a religious coloring book, a copy of the Koran, and C4 explosives. He sat down, placed the bag beneath him, announced in perfect Hebrew that he needed to go to the restroom, and ran outside. Fifteen seconds later an explosion killed 227 Jewish men, women, and children. One survivor was the soldier outside the synagogue who happened to see the child run outside. Out of curiosity he followed the child, felt the explosion behind him, then chased down the child. It was later that night the truth came out.

Israel's response was swift. They kept the Muslim child in custody and found out the entire plot. Within hours Israeli soldiers were evacuating every Muslim from Jerusalem and arresting those who resisted. They finally had world opinion on their side. The Great Atrocity was going to be avenged with the blood of the culprits.

The entire Muslim world reacted decisively. Seven Arab states announced that they were mobilizing against Israel. Israel didn't wait. Her jets were in the air and laying waste to those seven Arab states. When the Arabs finally were able to bomb Tel Aviv and Jerusalem, they also wreaked havoc. Many died in these air strikes. In the end, Israel prevailed because its response was so swift and decisive.

As the Israelis and Arabs buried their dead, Israel cleared the Temple Mount and began building the Third Temple, or what is also known as the Tribulation Temple.

Explaining Away the Rapture

We've already looked at one possible explanation the world will give for the disappearances that occur at the rapture: the possibility that a biological agent was used to wipe out those who had some kind of genetic "weakness." It's very likely there will be a number of theories abut what happened. Let's consider another one, which is likely to come from the religious front.

Those affiliated with the New Age movement may say that the people who vanished were spiritual individuals who were called up into the heavens to fight the forces of evil. They may claim that the New Age believers still on earth are the prophesied 144,000 saints of Revelation 7:4 and 14:1. They may say that the time had finally come for the forces of good upon the earth to take control and eliminate the forces of evil. They could declare we are now living in the "Millennial Age of Enlightenment" in this age of Aquarius. Rather than call the losses the Great Atrocity, they would call it "the Harvest."

Whatever the case, the fact that New Age followers have a nebulous spiritual worldview will appeal to many people. Because New Age proponents are popular and vocal, the world may feel their spiritual explanation for the disappearances is the best answer. We might even see the United Nations step forward and say something to this effect:

> "Science cannot comfort us. Politics cannot calm us. Explanations cannot convince us. But most of all, conflicts cannot break us. We must band together in trust to rebuild our broken lives and heal our nations. Providence has handed us many blows. Let it be our choice as a World People to overcome this adversity. Providence has called us to live in peace. Let us embrace without fear. Providence has provided us with the worldwide will of the people to unite and uplift the spirit of mankind. Let us not turn against our own mission. Now is the time to come together and become one. War no more."

The United Nations' Plan for the Millennium

If you think that the scenario described above is not possible, think again. Some people find it hard to believe that the United Nations has a goal of a developing single world government. The fact is, the United Nations threatens "dire consequences" for those who oppose this goal.

The following heading and the paragraphs that follow are from www.millenniumforum.org:

> We, 1,350 representatives of over 1,000 non-governmental organizations (NGOs) and other civil society organizations from more than 100 countries, have gathered at the United Nations (UN) Headquarters in New York from 22–26 May 2000 to build upon a common vision and the work begun at civil society conferences and the UN world conferences of the 1990s, to draw the attention of governments to the urgency of implementing the commitments they

have made, and to channel our collective energies by reclaiming globalization for and by the people.

Our vision is of a world that is human-centered and genuinely democratic, where all human beings are full participants and determine their own destinies. In our vision we are one human family, in all our diversity, living on one common homeland and sharing a just, sustainable and peaceful world, guided by universal principles of democracy, equality, inclusion, voluntarism, non-discrimination and participation by all persons, men and women, young and old, regardless of race, faith, disability, sexual orientation, ethnicity or nationality. It is a world where peace and human security, as envisioned in the principles of the United Nations Charter, replace armaments, violent conflict and wars. It is a world where everyone lives in a clean environment with a fair distribution of the earth's resources. Our vision includes a special role for the dynamism of young people and the experience of the elderly and reaffirms the universality, indivisibility and interdependence of all human rights—civil, political, economic, social and cultural.

Globalization should be made to work for the benefit of everyone: eradicate poverty and hunger globally; establish peace globally; ensure the protection and promotion of human rights globally; ensure the protection of our global environment; enforce social standards in the workplace globally....This can happen only if global corporations, international financial and trade institutions and governments are subject to effective democratic control by the people. We see a strengthened and democratized United Nations and a vibrant civil society as guarantors of this accountability. And we issue a warning: If the architects of globalization are not held to account, this will not simply be unjust; the edifice will crumble with dire consequences for everyone. In the end, the wealthy will find no refuge, as intolerance, disease, environmental devastation, war, social disintegration and political instability spread.[3]

It is interesting for us to note that the NGOs (non-governmental organizations) that are pushing for globalized government through the United Nations have no real standing as voting members. That is, unelected officials decide our destinies, and this kind of rulership is becoming increasingly common throughout the world. Even in the United States we have myriads of bureaucrats who run the country from administration to administration, not particularly concerned with who is in office from term to term.

Ten Keys to the Antichrist's Identity

The one-world government, of course, will have a figurehead, a ruler who oversees the implementation of the one-world government's policies. The Bible gives us at least ten keys to identifying this coming world ruler. We have enough details to give us a general idea of who he will be when Satan inspires him to make his move onto the world scene. These clues also make it clear that only one person in history will fit this description. There have been many prototypes, but there will only be one Antichrist.

1. He will rise to power in the last days: "Later in the time of wrath [the time of the end] ...a stern-faced king, a master of intrigue, will arise" (Daniel 8:19,23).

2. He will rule the whole world: "He was given authority over every tribe, people, language and nation" (Revelation 13:7).

3. His headquarters will be in Rome: "The beast, which you saw, once was, now is not, and will come up out of the Abyss....The seven heads are seven hills on which the woman sits" (Revelation 17:8-9). The seven hills spoken of in this verse are commonly believed to refer to the city of Rome, which sits upon seven hills.

4. He will be intelligent and persuasive: "The other horn...looked more imposing than the others and...had eyes and a mouth that spoke boastfully" (Daniel 7:20).

5. He will rule by international consent: "The ten horns you saw are ten kings....They have one purpose and will give their power and authority to the beast" (Revelation 17:12-13).

6. He will rule by deception: "He will become very strong....and will succeed in whatever he does....He will cause deceit to prosper, and he will consider himself superior" (Daniel 8:24-25).

7. He will control the global economy: "He also forced everyone, small and great, rich and poor, free and slave, to receive a mark on his right hand or on his forehead, so that no one could buy or sell unless he had the mark, which is the name of the beast or the number of his name" (Revelation 13:16-17).

8. He will make a peace treaty with Israel: "He will confirm a covenant with many for one 'seven.' In the middle of the 'seven' he will put an end to sacrifice and offering" (Daniel 9:27).

9. He will break the treaty and invade Israel: "The people of the ruler who will come will destroy the

city and the sanctuary. The end will come like a flood: War will continue until the end, and the desolations have been decreed" (Daniel 9:26).

10. He will claim to be God: "He will oppose and will exalt himself over everything that is called God or is worshiped, so that he sets himself up in God's temple, proclaiming himself to be God" (2 Thessalonians 2:4).

There are many other details given in the Bible regarding the person we commonly call the Antichrist. But the general picture is that of a European who rises to power over the Western world. Whether he is Jewish or Gentile is not entirely clear. What is clear, however, is that he will control the last great bastion of Gentile world power. From his base in the West, he will extend his control over the entire world. For all practical purposes, he will administrate the world government and the global economy with assistance from the leader of the one-world religion (Revelation 13:11-18). He may be alive somewhere in the world; only time will reveal his true identity.

When he does come to power, the Antichrist will promise world peace through a series of international alliances, treaties, and agreements. Despite his promises of peace, however, his international polices will inevitably plunge the world into the greatest war of all time.

13

The Wave Comes Crashing Down

Future Wave

Enter Story

Future Story: The World as One

The last year had been a wake-up call not only for the entire world, but for the Jewish people in particular. The Third Temple was now under construction, and the United Nations had signed a Declaration of World Peace, with the full blessing of the Israelis, to make Jerusalem the Holy City for the United Nations and to place it in the careful custody of an international board of directors. There would be no more fighting over this Holy City, and the full force of the United Nations would be sure of that.

The Muslims found the terms agreeable since the city was no longer under Jewish control, and they were able to have their mosques. The Jews were content to have a city of peace and the Holy Temple near completion. The dream they had held to for many, many generations was finally coming true. It wasn't an ideal situation, but it was an attractive set of tradeoffs, and Jews from all over the world were heading to the Holy Land in greater numbers than ever before.

As a result of the so-called Harvest, churches all around the world that had lost many members were coming together to form a more united denomination. A strong leader who emerged in Europe called for the World Community to cast out their doubts and to welcome the entire world into the Fellowship of Man. He pushed for the world to unite politically under the auspices of the United Nations and spiritually under the Worldwide Millennium Church. There soon appeared at bookstores everywhere *The Millennium Testament*.

Soon, the spiritual rhetoric of the Millennium Church won the minds of men. *The Millennium Testament*, which covered 2,000 years of history, spoke glowingly of how the world had come through trial after trial successfully. The world had managed to survive the Dark Ages, eliminate slavery, defeat fascist dictators, and cure the bulk of humanity's ailments.

The Millennium Testament held out a message of hope for all people. It aligned itself with the mission of the United Nations, addressing the need to eradicate poverty and hunger globally, to ensure the dissident rights of those who choose alternative lifestyles, and to protect the weak from those who would use and abuse them. It contained the writings of great minds from every corner of the world—no religion or philosophy was left out. It was inclusion and tolerance of others as had never been seen before.

The Origins of Globalization

The prospect of a one-world government has been raised numerous times by many Bible prophecy experts and needs to be taken seriously. With the advent of a United Nations that now has military backing that it uses readily, with the new World Court that claims dominion over all nations, with the banking power and economic lordship of the World Bank and the International Monetary Fund (IMF), with the growing power and cooperation of the European Commonwealth, with the advent of more stringent government controls upon the citizens of all nations, and with the breakdown of political barriers that formerly hindered financiers and multinational corporations, the stage is set for the world's peoples to lose their sovereignty as individuals and as nations.

While we do not advocate any particular conspiracy theories, we do want to point out that a movement toward world government is the goal of many businessmen and preeminent leaders. One of former President Bill Clinton's mentors, the late Carroll Quigley, a highly esteemed Georgetown University professor and author, wrote a book titled *Tragedy and Hope* (1966), which gives us an insider's view of the capabilities and goals of a world financial system. In the book, he makes the following points:[1]

- There exists an international network that wishes to remain unknown.[2]

- Professor Quigley was a supporter who believed the network's role in history was significant and should be known.[3]

- This secretive network organized in Britain and her dependencies as Round Table Groups and the Royal Institute of International Affairs.[4]

- This network is organized as the Council on Foreign Relations in New York.[5]

Perhaps the most worrisome of all of Professor Quigley's summations about this network regards their financial goals:

> In addition to these pragmatic goals, the powers of financial capitalism had another far-reaching aim, nothing less than to create a world system of financial control in private hands able to dominate the political system of each country and the economy of the world as a whole. This system was to be controlled in a feudalist fashion by the central banks of the world acting in concert, by secret agreements arrived at in frequent meetings and conferences.[6]

We have absolutely no reason to doubt the authenticity of Professor Quigley's statements. Ongoing research, which may result in another book, does nothing less than validate the fact that world bankers are taking greater control of the world through money. Mark Rizzo of Freedom Flyer Ministries often works with law enforcement agencies and teaches recruits at the FBI Academy. He shares with us that the criminal investigative process is simple: *Follow the money and the power.*

The United Nations funds the International Monetary Fund (IMF). The IMF is engaged in lending money to nations that are poor and generally cannot even afford to pay the interest on the loans. The IMF then forces financial adjustment plans and austerity measures upon those countries that are having difficulty servicing their debt. You can find out more about the IMF at www.imf.org.

The Bank for International Settlements (BIS) was established in 1930 "to promote the cooperation of central banks and to provide additional facilities for international financial operations,"[7] according to article three of their original statutes. The BIS is made up of the Central Banks of many countries, and one of their major aims is to foster international financial stability through cooperation.

The Organization for Economic Cooperation and Development (OECD) is an offshoot from the Marshall Plan that was implemented after World War II for the purpose of reconstructing Europe. The OECD groups 29 member countries in an organization that provides governments a setting in which to discuss, develop, and perfect economic and social policy. They compare experiences, seek answers to common problems, and work to coordinate domestic and international policies that, in today's globalized world, must form a web of even practice across nations. Their exchanges may also lead to agreements to act in a formal way.[8]

The World Bank is similar in nature to the International Monetary Fund but is made up of several smaller development funds. The primary focus of the World Bank is reformative in nature. They are a world advocate for human rights and they use their power to lend to get results. They also engage in pressuring countries to conform to their ideals by withholding funds, if need be. Founded in 1944, the World Bank group consists of five closely associated institutions: the International Bank for Reconstruction and Development (IBRD), the International Development Association (IDA), the International Finance Corporation (IFC), the Multilateral Investment Guarantee Agency (MIGA), and the International Center for Settlement of Investment Disputes (ICSID).[9]

These groups do not have evil intents or designs; certainly the vast majority of individuals working within these organizations are well-meaning people who are trying to make the world a better place. However, their worldwide reach and influence makes them likely agents for use by anyone endeavoring to forge a one-world government. Also, many of the countries that are indebted to these international banks have been perched precariously on the edge of financial collapse year after year, only to be propped up by more loans. That arrangement puts the banks in a position of power over these nations.

What's more, there is a serious problem with shuffling money around in an attempt to make these debtor nations appear liquid. What would happen if there were significant economic collapse? *Time* magazine made an interesting observation that should speak volumes to Christian readers familiar with the prophecies regarding the end times: "History's great inflations have almost always been followed by a dictator who promised, among other things, to restore the currency's value. Napoleon, Hitler and Mao Tse-tung all rode to power on the back of hyperinflation."[10] In fact, the Bible predicts horrible inflation in the last days:

> When the Lamb opened the third seal, I heard the third living creature say, "Come!" I looked, and there before me was a black horse! Its rider was holding a pair of scales in his hand. Then I heard what sounded like a voice among the four living creatures, saying, "A quart of wheat for a day's wages, and three quarts of barley for a day's wages, and do not damage the oil and the wine!" (Revelation 6:5-6).

Future Story: Man's Temple and God's Temple

The Mideast War had a great effect upon Gerald Litman, being that he was Jewish and had tracked his lineage back to the tribe of Benjamin many years ago. Of course, he had already been devastated by the loss of his family. For a while, he had been unable to go back to work. His wealth lost meaning to him, and he sold out all of his financial holdings and started living off of the money. He shunned his longtime friends and acquaintances and kept to himself. He was in that spot the devil wanted him in—feeding off the bottom of his soul, isolated in his own torment. Gerald started drinking heavily and using drugs. He knew they weren't the answer, but he didn't know where else to turn for relief from his pain.

One day, one of Gerald's old friends from TrafficAir called upon him and immediately realized Gerald needed help. He told Gerald that TrafficAir had been working on a new implant that helped many people who were struggling with similar problems. Since Gerald's departure, TrafficAir had developed LifeLine II and successfully negotiated the strategic alliances they needed to go front-and-center on the world stage with their new product.

The LifeLine II implant could locate people as needed, monitor their medical condition, steer them away from danger, give them directions, communicate with them, give them any data they needed instantaneously, entertain them, approve their expenditures, remind them of their appointments, and even give them a good vibe.

The technology was rather complex, but TrafficAir was able to bring together several different disciplines and unite them into this one incredible tool. The main device people bought was called LifeLine II and consisted of a small microchip that was implanted into their right hand between the thumb and the index finger via a routine vaccination. They were able to have the microchip injected painlessly at any doctor's office, and each LifeLine II had a unique identification number—actually a set of three numbers of six digits each.

After a few days, the microchip would become tethered into the user's nerve endings. This would then activate the microchip, which was said to promise happiness.

Along with the LifeLine II vaccination, a person could purchase additional equipment that offered more benefits. Many companies, including TrafficAir, marketed what were called *Lenses*. These looked just like eyeglasses and were used in lieu of eyeglasses for those people whose vision was failing. But the Lenses did much more. They also had a microphone built into the frame that could receive voice commands and transfer them to the LifeLine II implant. Then the LifeLine II implant would send the command to your provider, who would then send back the requested programming. Sometimes it would result in a simple nerve stimulation, which would be administered by the LifeLine II implant. Other programming and entertainment could be viewed on the Lenses and heard on the earpiece that was integrated on the frame of the Lenses.

At first, only the wealthy could afford this. Gerald listened and was impressed as his old friends at TrafficAir praised their LifeLine II implants. He decided to give it a try. Gerald received the vaccination, and from that time onward, his life changed. He purchased programming that stimulated his natural hormones to eliminate his craving for drugs and alcohol. Interestingly, that same stimulation also gave him that feeling of ease that he had initially enjoyed when he started using alcohol and drugs.

The LifeLine II implant, coupled with the new understanding of the human genome, made it possible to give people what they had wanted all along: a sense of ease and comfort. Many others enjoyed the benefits of the implant, which seemed to be the solution that would bring many people's problems to an end. The entire world celebrated. Gerald even felt good enough to join the Worldwide Millennium Church, which had organized after the departure of all the people taken during the Harvest.

Ensnared by the Beast

For many years, writers, lecturers, and Bible teachers have given various opinions about the mark of the beast and the nature of the beast. There has been much speculation about a supercomputer being one of the two beasts mentioned in Revelation chapter 13. One hypothesis has been that a computer, or series of computers, will issue an identification number to every person born on the planet. This number might be similar to the Social Security number we use in the United States, which is nine digits long and has three parts.

From the first three digits of a person's Social Security number you can determine where a person lived when they were assigned their number. It is only the first three digits that are of any value; the rest of the number is designed to specify a particular individual. With this nine-digit arrangement and the use of the numerals from zero to nine, it is possible for the United States government to number over nine billion people. That type of numbering capacity should last for some time.

There has been speculation that a one-world government would need a greater numbering capacity and thus might use a three-part number with each part having six digits.

This would dovetail with the prophecy concerning the three sixes:

> This calls for wisdom. If anyone has insight, let him calculate the number of the beast, for it is man's number. His number is 666 (Revelation 13:18).

A three-part number with six digits in each part would allow over 999 quadrillion people to be numbered—more than enough to number every person on earth for the next 2,000 years. By the way, keep in mind that we have already created microchip implants for animals that stay charged without an external power source, and these have the ability to number up to 15 digits. A 15-digit number, given the world population of six billion souls, would enable us to number the entire world population thousands of times over. Indeed, with the four billion livestock animals in the world feeding six billion people who own 200 million household pets, we can still use the microchip implants to our hearts' desire and keep track of everybody and their animals for the millennia to come.

Going back to the possibility that the beast might be a computer, our technological resources make that a possibility. However, keep in mind that the Bible says people will "worship" the image of the beast:

> Then I saw another beast, coming out of the earth. He had two horns like a lamb, but he spoke like a dragon. He exercised all the authority of the first beast on his behalf, and made the earth and its inhabitants worship the first beast, whose fatal wound had been healed. And he performed great and miraculous signs, even causing fire to come down from heaven to earth in full view of men. Because of the signs he was given power to do on behalf of the first beast, he deceived the inhabitants of the earth. He ordered them to set up an image in

honor of the beast who was wounded by the sword and yet lived. He was given power to give breath to the image of the first beast, so that it could speak and cause all who refused to worship the image to be killed (Revelation 13:11-15).

In this context, the translation from the Greek word for "worship" should be interpreted to mean "pay homage to" or "to bow before." The passage is not talking about the kind of worship we have for God. Satan doesn't need for us to worship him; he only needs for us *not* to worship God. Thus, misguided humanity might be inclined to pay homage to the beast, especially if not doing so resulted in starvation or death!

Could the Internet be the beast? Could our constant attention to e-mail be the homage that we pay? Certainly many of us are fond of our technology and the expedient communications that result from it. But there are other technological marvels that are much more seductive than computers. How Satan will use these to ensnare us may not yet be fully clear. What is clear is that we are well on the way to entrapment.

Almost all of us have at least one television in our home. Television has become so important to modern life that whole families can hardly imagine living without it. It baby-sits our children when we are busy, teaches them their letters and numbers, educates us with documentaries, informs us with news, inspires and challenges us with good programming, preoccupies us with live events, and hypnotizes us with entertainment. Those who have cable connections or satellite feeds have dozens of viewing options at their disposal 24 hours a day. For some, even that isn't enough!

How much more would our families find television indispensable if it also worked as an intercom within the house, or provided televideo communications with our distant relatives? What if we received our mail through our television and we could decide, within seconds, what was worthy of our attention? What if we could play video games against a good friend anywhere in the world? What if the programming we received could be ordered in advance so that we could watch it at our convenience instead of watching it at a fixed time simultaneously with everyone else? What if we could do our grocery shopping and clothes shopping by television? And not be limited to the products featured on the TV shopping networks, but, rather, be able to request viewings only of the products in which we are interested? What if you could do your taxes, pay your bills, track your investments, and do your banking all with one gadget? Even better, what if you could do all of the above from anywhere in the world?

Worldwide Internet Access

Earlier, we mentioned a TV commercial in which an English-speaking man is in a park in Europe trading American stocks. He is looking at the stock quotes on the lenses of his eyeglasses and speaking his orders into a microphone. Imagine also being able to conduct video conferences from anywhere in the world to anywhere else in the world, and being able to take care of your banking, shopping, appointments, and more, all using one device?

In relation to worldwide Internet access, it's important to note that the United Nations funds the Sustainable Development Networking Program (SDNP). Part of the purpose of that program is spelled out on their website as follows:

> In this light, it is evident that the "Internet Revolution"...created new issues and problems in DCs [developing countries], issues and problems that need to be specifically addressed by developmental

organizations and institutions. These are some of the issues that the Sustainable Development Networking Program has been addressing since its inception, by operating at the country level, launching and supporting local Internet sites, and building national capacities and knowledge resources.[11]

Recently the SDNP reported that by 2005 everyone in the world should have access to the Internet even though it may require a short sojourn to the nearest access point. Chuck Lankester has been the director of the SDNP since 1992. He said, "It is incumbent on us, and we feel that it is entirely possible...that by the end of 2004 a farmer in Saharan Africa should be able to get to a point of access, let's say in half a day's walk or riding on a bullock cart."

While much is being done to bring Internet access to the whole world, the "digital divide" between the United States and other countries is still large. Even Europe lags behind, and many third-world nations are still not able to afford the infrastructure it takes to provide anything more than very limited Internet access. We can expect that much will be done in the days ahead to get the rest of the world on the Internet.

Future Story: The Millennial Mind

It has been a couple years since Gerald Litman lost his family. During that time, technology made some great strides forward, and the world continued to change rapidly.

Gerald has also had the LifeLine II implanted in his hand, joined the Worldwide Millennium Church, and returned to running his company, TrafficAir. Life had settled into a routine once again, and he was enjoying the peace and prosperity that followed the horrible Mideast war. There were still some major problems with the overall human conditions around the world, but the United Nations and the Worldwide Millennium Church were doing a fair job of keeping the lid on during those tumultuous times.

The LifeLine II, meanwhile, continued to grow in its capabilities and popularity. Gerald's firm had put together strategic alliances that made the LifeLine II programming essential to people all over the world. There were hardly any areas of living that the LifeLine II couldn't make better. One of the more recent developments had to do with linking everybody into the Millennial Mind, or global brain. Whatever someone needed was provided, courtesy of the unelected elite of the United Nations and the Worldwide Millennium Church.

The Millennial Mind

The following is from *The Global Brain*, a book by Peter Russell:

> The interlinking of humanity that began with the emergence of language has now progressed to the point where information can be transmitted to anyone, anywhere, at the speed of light. Billions of messages continually shuttling back and forth, in an

ever-growing web of communication, linking the billions of minds of humanity together into a single system.

We have already noted that there are, very approximately, the same number of nerve cells in a human brain as there are human minds on the planet. And there are also some interesting similarities between the way the human brain grows and the way in which humanity is evolving. The embryonic human brain passes through two major phases of development. The first is a massive explosion in the number of nerve cells. Starting eight weeks after conception, the number of neurons explodes, increasing by many millions each hour. After five weeks, however, the process slows down, almost as rapidly as it started. The first stage of brain development, the proliferation of cells, is now complete. At this stage the fetus has most of the nerve cells it will have for the rest of its life.

The brain then proceeds to the second phase of its development, as billions of isolated nerve cells begin making connections with each other, sometimes growing out fibers to connect with cells on the other side of the brain. By the time of birth, a typical nerve cell may communicate directly with several thousand other cells. The growth of the brain after birth consists of the further proliferation of connections. By the time of adulthood many nerve cells are making direct connections with as many as a quarter of a million other cells.

Similar trends can be observed in human society. For the last few centuries the number of "cells" in the "embryonic global brain" has been proliferating. But today population growth is slowing, and at the same time we are moving into the next phase—the linking

of the billions of human minds into a single integrated network. The more complex our global
telecommunication capabilities become the more
human society is beginning to look like a planetary
nervous system. The global brain is beginning to
function.[12]

The Millennial Mind, or global brain, will be a collection
of data on all of the world's people. It will also be a central
repository for world knowledge, with links to all other
human beings, businesses, and institutions. If the Millennial
Mind does not have the information you need within its
own database, it will redirect you at lightning speed to
retrieve the information from somewhere.

From that perspective, the Millennial Mind is like the
human mind. We are limited in our knowledge, but we are
never limited in the knowledge that is available to us
through our reaching out to other sources. Currently we
reach out to periodicals, books, the Internet, or other people.
In the case of the Millennial Mind, we will voice our
request, it will search its database for the exact keyword
matches, and it will present us with the results.

In addition, the Millennial Mind will already know our
past history and prioritize the search results based upon our
past requests.

Monitoring Your Every Move

For those of us accustomed to individual liberties, one of the
most difficult issues regarding the global brain is relin-
quishing our privacy. But for the good of society we will be
asked to do so. After all, isn't the welfare of the general
public more important than any one individual's rights?

Suppose there is a known terrorist organization located
in Afghanistan. Wouldn't it make sense for us to monitor all

of their communications? What about that 34-year-old Syrian foreign exchange student at UCLA that the terrorist group keeps calling? Should we monitor his communications too? That's where Echelon steps in.

Patrick S. Poole reports:

> ECHELON is actually a vast network of electronic spy stations located around the world and maintained by five countries: the U.S., England, Canada, Australia, and New Zealand. These countries, bound together in a still-secret agreement called UKUSA, spy on each other's citizens by intercepting and gathering electronic signals of almost every telephone call, fax transmission and e-mail message transmitted around the world daily. These signals are fed through the massive supercomputers of the NSA to look for certain keywords called the ECHELON "dictionaries."[13]

In a *WorldNetDaily* report on November 12, 1998, Stephan Archer said:

> Once these spy facilities collect the phone calls, e-mails, and faxes, of virtually everyone on earth, the Echelon system sorts them through a kind of filter system known as the Echelon dictionary. This dictionary looks for "flag" words in all of the transmitted communication. While it lets a majority of all collected material pass through its filter, it tags those that may pose a threat and tracks all subsequent communication coming from the source of the original "flagged" message.[14]

It is comforting to know that the government is hard at work monitoring our enemies. But what happens when the citizen becomes the "enemy"?

The Beast Rears Its Ugly Head

Gerald Litman kept thinking about moving to Israel. It seemed like everything was happening there. The Third Temple had been built. There was always talk of holy men being there. All of this was at the New Jerusalem, which had been designated as the headquarters of the new world religion by the United Nations. Besides, Gerald was Jewish and he could still remember his parents' and grandparents' conversations about how wonderful it would be for the Jews to be able to return to their homeland and live in peace.

One day Gerald met with a highly placed representative of the United Nations. This man was the personal aide of the Secretary General. The United Nations was about to implement a requirement that member nations conduct all their commerce through the United Nations' controlled Millennial Mind. The reason was that the United Nations needed a reliable tax base, and a small international sales tax base would work best. The Secretary General had already met with all the key heads of state and won their approval. All that remained was to make the LifeLine II a requirement for every citizen in any member nation.

The United Nations wanted to sign a contract with TrafficAir that would supply the LifeLine II at a reduced cost with a guarantee of immediate sales in the hundreds of billions of dollars. This was incredible news! It would make TrafficAir the most successful company on the face of the earth! Litman certainly didn't need the money, but the thought of the power associated with such an arrangement intrigued him.

One of TrafficAir's critical suppliers had its headquarters in Jerusalem. Gerald flew there to work out the feasibility and timeline for the increased production of the LifeLine II. While there, he ran across a curious sight, which is described for us in Revelation 11:3-6:

> I will give power to my two witnesses, and they will prophesy for 1,260 days, clothed in sackcloth. These are the two olive trees and the two lampstands that stand before the Lord of the earth. If anyone tries to harm them, fire comes from their mouths and devours their enemies. This is how anyone who wants to harm them must die. These men have power to shut up the sky so that it will not rain during the time they are prophesying; and they have power to turn the waters into blood and to strike the earth with every kind of plague as often as they want (Revelation 11:3-6).

The Turning Point

Gerald Litman, now in Old Jerusalem, asked his guide about the strange man speaking a mixture of Hebrew and English. The man was dressed like a pilgrim of some sort and seemed to speak with authority and power. He always had a good-sized crowd around him, and many people were also praying and talking with one another.

Litman's guide told him that the man suffered from Jerusalem Syndrome, a mental delusion that he is a character from the Torah. The guide explained that Jerusalem has always attracted psychotics who thought they were on a mission from God. He said it was unusual for such a man to draw such a large crowd, but that he was particularly good at it. The guide added that there was another fellow on the other side of Old Jerusalem who was just as good.

Litman pretended to look disinterested, but deep inside, he was very curious. The people around the man didn't act like they were merely being entertained. They seemed to be earnestly affected by this man, and the man seemed to have a strange power about him.

Later that night Gerald went for a walk around Old Jerusalem. He heard the commotion of a public gathering and saw what looked like lightning in the sky. He hurried over to see the second man in sackcloth that his guide had mentioned. All around, people were praying, singing, counseling, watching, and listening. The man glowed as if there were a great light behind him, and lightning came from the sky above. But there was no rain and there had been no rain for quite some time.

Gerald's pulse quickened and he could feel his heart beating faster. He moved closer, and as he did so, his doubts disappeared and his heart calmed. Gerald didn't understand why, but he felt safe. He listened to every word. At first the man spoke mostly English, but then he spoke more and more Hebrew. Litman wondered briefly how it was that he could understand every word the man spoke in Hebrew even though his own knowledge of Hebrew was modest at best.

The strange man spoke again: "I have not made trouble for Israel, but you and your father's family have. You have abandoned the LORD's commands and have followed the Baals. How long will you waver between two opinions? If the LORD is God, follow him; but if Baal is God, follow him. I am the only one of the LORD's prophets left, but Baal has four hundred and fifty prophets. O LORD, God of Abraham, Isaac and Israel, let it be known today that you are God in Israel and that I am your servant and have done all these things at your command." Then the sky lit up again, and Gerald fell to his knees. He understood these words were the words of Elijah, which he had learned when he was a youngster in Hebrew school.

A rabbi walked over to Gerald and asked him, "Are you ready to receive Christ into your heart as your Messiah?" Gerald looked up at the face marked by compassion, and cried out, "Yes Lord, redeem me. I have sinned against you and all of humanity. Forgive me and accept me and lead me."

The Bible's Warning

While we have followed Gerald Litman as a fictional character in the storylines of the last few chapters, the scenario just presented, with the prophets in Old Jerusalem, is not fictional. These two prophets will testify of God for many days. Revelation 11:7-13 tells us what will happen at the end of their ministry:

> When they have finished their testimony, the beast that comes up from the Abyss will attack them, and overpower and kill them. Their bodies will lie in the street of the great city, which is figuratively called Sodom and Egypt, where also their Lord was crucified. For three and a half days men from every people, tribe, language and nation will gaze on their bodies and refuse them burial. The inhabitants of the earth will gloat over them and will celebrate by sending each other gifts, because these two prophets had tormented those who live on the earth. But after

the three and a half days a breath of life from God entered them, and they stood on their feet, and terror struck those who saw them. Then they heard a loud voice from heaven saying to them, "Come up here." And they went up to heaven in a cloud, while their enemies looked on. At that very hour there was a severe earthquake and a tenth of the city collapsed. Seven thousand people were killed in the earthquake, and the survivors were terrified and gave glory to the God of heaven.

Future Story: Underground

Gerald Litman, now a Christian, started to fight against the very system he had created. He no longer desired to serve man, but wanted only to serve God. He went to a Christian doctor in Jerusalem and had his LifeLine II implant removed. In removing the implant, both he and the doctor were risking their lives.

Meanwhile, the two witnesses in Old Jerusalem had been assassinated in public, and their bodies were left where they fell. For three days, the whole world celebrated the deaths of the two men. But miraculously, life entered back into their bodies, and they stood up and ascended into heaven in a cloud. Some even said that they heard a great voice from heaven calling the witnesses by name into heaven. Gerald knew this would happen because he had recently found a copy of the Bible and started reading what it said about the last days in the book of Revelation. The work of the witnesses was done, and those who remained—including Gerald—were fully committed to fighting the very evil they had once promoted.

Gerald knew his money would no longer do him any good, so he converted his savings into hard goods as quickly as possible. He immediately returned to Los Angeles and got busy. Gerald used part of his wealth to set up nearly 300 computer labs around the world. They were, in effect, cells, with one not knowing the location of the other. They were located in the homes of dedicated believers who shared news and the Good News with each other daily. The purpose of the labs was to maintain communications over what was now called "the fishnet," an Internet alternative for Christians. They used the airwaves to communicate and they changed their frequencies daily so that it was difficult for their enemies to track them down.

The reports were horrendous from all around the world, and every believer knew they were living in the last days. The Tribulation was occurring right before their eyes, and many knew that most of them would not survive the horrific days ahead.

14

The Millennial Wave

During the Tribulation, people on earth will face the most horrible suffering, warfare, and disaster the world has ever known. Jesus predicted this time, saying, "For then there will be great distress, unequaled from the beginning of the world until now—and never to be equaled again. If those days had not been cut short, no one would survive, but for the sake of the elect those days will be shortened" (Matthew 24:21-22).

At the end of the Tribulation, Jesus the Messiah will return to this earth in the same way as He left over 2,000 years ago. When Jesus left, He ascended in a cloud as His disciples watched. Then suddenly two men dressed in white stood beside the disciples. "Men of Galilee," they said, "why do you stand here looking into the sky? This same Jesus, who has been taken from you into heaven, will come back in the same way you have seen him go into heaven" (Acts 1:10-11).

Jesus ascended into heaven alone, but when He returns, He will have all His holy angels and the raptured, glorified church with Him: "The armies of heaven were following

229

him, riding on white horses and dressed in fine linen, white and clean" (Revelation 19:14).

The final battle of Armageddon, which will culminate in the defeat of the Antichrist's massive army, will result in the complete collapse of all the world's war machines—a collapse that will last 1,000 years. Jesus will annihilate the conquest-minded people of the earth in one swift move. This could involve as many as 200,000,000 soldiers. Who then will be left to clean up the earth and continue the advance of civilization? Will everyone left on earth enter Jesus' millennial kingdom?

After Jesus liberates the holy city from the Antichrist and removes the abomination of desolation, He will set up His throne. The first thing on His agenda will be to gather the survivors unto Himself to witness a major event—a wedding banquet. We know this because of an interesting parable Jesus taught in Matthew chapter 22 about a wedding banquet. Let's look at that parable in detail.

The Future Wedding Feast

Christ's Ministry on This Earth

"The kingdom of heaven is like a king who prepared a wedding banquet for his son. He sent his servants to those who had been invited to the banquet to tell them to come, but they refused to come" (Matthew 22:2-3).

The fall of man did not take God by surprise. In His eternal plan God, the King of the universe, would send His Son to this earth to die for the sins of the world. Christ's main focus and message while on this earth was for the Jews, His chosen people or bride, to come to a wedding. God wanted His bride, but His bride would not come: "He came to that which was his own, but his own did not receive him."

After His death, burial and resurrection, Christ went back into heaven without a bride.

The Church Age

"Then he [the king] sent some more servants and said, 'Tell those who have been invited that I have prepared my dinner: My oxen and fattened cattle have been butchered, and everything is ready. Come to the wedding banquet.' But they paid no attention and went off—one to his field, another to his business" (Matthew 22:4-5).

For 2,000 years the people of the world, including the Jewish people, have continued to be invited by God to His Son's wedding banquet. This message has been delivered in tent revivals, churches in every corner of the globe, citywide crusades, television, radio, and now the Internet. Billions of people, both Jew and Gentile, have heard a clear gospel message and either made light of it and turned away or have accepted it and become Christians.

The Tribulation Period

"The rest ['remnant' in KJV] *seized his servants, mistreated them and killed them. The king was enraged. He sent his army and destroyed those murderers and burned their city"* (Matthew 22:6-7).

If the parable follows history in chronological order, then Matthew 22:6-7 could refer to the Tribulation period. According to Revelation 7, the witness of the 144,000 converted Jews will lead multitudes of people to salvation during the Tribulation. During the first three-and-a-half years of the Tribulation the world will experience somewhat peaceful conditions as the Antichrist sets up his one-world government and one-world religion. However, God's judgments will be falling upon this earth during this time and millions of people will be killed. At the midpoint of the Tribulation, the Antichrist will break his treaty with Israel and force everyone to receive his mark or face the consequences. It is at this time that the "remnant" or "rest" of the people who are left will seize and persecute those who refused to take the mark. Some Christians will be thrown into prison, some will be killed, and some will have to go into a survival mode for the remainder of the Tribulation.

Christ's Return at the End of the Tribulation Period

"Then he said to his servants, 'The wedding banquet is ready, but those I invited did not deserve to come. Go to the street corners and invite to the banquet anyone you find.'" (Matthew 22:8-9).

At the end of the Tribulation, Christ will return to earth with His bride, the church. He will come back to a world that is ravaged and nearly destroyed. The disasters and destruction will have brought the world to a standstill. But, in every corner of the earth there will be survivors—some in underground shelters, some in caves, some in makeshift huts, and some who during this time managed to live in affluence because they followed the now-collapsed programs set up by the Antichrist. How will Christ get the word to them that a new government has taken over?

The answer may be in Matthew 22:10, the next verse in the parable: "So the servants went out into the streets and gathered all the people they could find, both good and bad, and the wedding hall was filled with guests" (Matthew 22:10). Who are these servants who went out into the highways? Could they be Christ's bride, the church? A closer look at these servants will tell us who they are as well as the identity of who they invited to attend the wedding feast.

Identifying the Bride of Christ

On the night before His crucifixion, Jesus promised His disciples that He was going to heaven to prepare a place for them. He said, "If I go and prepare a place for you, I will come back and take you to be with me that you also may be where I am" (John 14:3). The apostle Paul also spoke of the great hope every believer can look forward to in the future: "Behold, I show you a mystery; we shall not all sleep [die], but we shall all be changed [resurrected, or raptured], in a moment, in the twinkling of an eye, at the last trump: for the trumpet shall sound, and the dead shall be raised incorruptible, and we shall be changed" (1 Corinthians 15:51-52 KJV).

Paul reiterates this same hope in 1 Thessalonians 4:13-17 when he comments about those believers who have already died and gone to heaven. He says,

> Brothers, we do not want you to be ignorant about those who fall asleep, or to grieve like the rest of men, who have no hope. We believe that Jesus died and rose again and so we believe that God will bring with Jesus those who have fallen asleep in him. According to the Lord's own word, we tell you that we who are still alive, who are left till the coming of the Lord, will certainly not precede those who have fallen asleep. For the Lord himself will come down from heaven, with a loud command, with the voice of the archangel and with the trumpet call of God, and the dead in Christ will rise first. After that, we who are still alive and are left will be caught up together with them in the clouds to meet the Lord in the air. And so we will be with the Lord forever.

The promise to return for the church (the believers of the church age) is the promise of the rapture. The rapture of the believer is part of the fixed plan of God. The only thing not known about this part of God's plan is the time. When

Revelation chapter 19 opens, the resurrected Christians have already received their rewards for their righteous works at the *bema* seat judgment, and we read about the church's marriage to Christ and a glorious marriage supper. The apostle John says "the wedding of the Lamb has come, and his bride has made herself ready" (Revelation 19:7).

John's detailed vision of the marriage supper includes a description of the bride's garment. She is dressed in "fine linen, bright and clean" (Revelation 19:8). Here the church is shown as completely cleansed through Christ's completed work on the cross. John also tells us that there are guests at this marriage supper. They are those "who are invited to the wedding supper of the Lamb" (Revelation 19:9). The guests at the wedding are the Tribulation martyrs, Old Testament saints, and the angelic hosts of heaven. While we will live with the Old Testament saints in the New Jerusalem, they are not part of the bride of Christ.

Identifying the Army of Heaven

Almost immediately after the wedding, John sees the armies of heaven that follow Jesus out to battle:

> I saw heaven standing open and there before me was a white horse, whose rider is called Faithful and True. With justice he judges and makes war. His eyes are like blazing fire, and on his head are many crowns. He has a name written on him that no one knows but he himself. He is dressed in a robe dipped in blood, and his name is the Word of God. The armies of heaven were following him, riding on white horses and dressed in fine linen, white and clean. Out of his mouth comes a sharp sword with which to strike down the nations. "He will rule them with an iron scepter." He treads the winepress of the fury of the wrath of God Almighty. On his robe and

on his thigh he has this name written: King of kings and Lord of lords. And I saw an angel standing in the sun, who cried in a loud voice to all the birds flying in midair, "Come, gather together for the great supper of God" (Revelation 19:11-17).

What a contrast to the wedding supper of the Lamb! These saints are probably the same ones seen at the marriage supper. They are clothed with the same white linen as we saw earlier at the wedding feast—a clean garment symbolic of their righteousness through the shed blood of Christ.

What Will We Be Like?

Our Resurrection Bodies

Bible teacher and prophecy expert Grant Jeffrey answers this question well when he says this:

> When Jesus rose from the dead and appeared to His disciples, His resurrected body was similar to, yet different from, His mortal body before His death on the cross. He still had flesh and bones, and His hands and feet carried the scars from the cross (Luke 24:39). Shortly after His resurrection he appeared to His disciples after walking through a closed door. There He met Thomas, who earlier said "I won't believe Jesus is risen until I see the nail prints in His hand and the wound in His side." Jesus walked up to Thomas and invited him to put his finger in the nail hole in His wrist and the gaping hole in His side (see John 20:27). Jesus even ate and drank with His disciples after His resurrection (John 21:12-14). Yet there was an indefinable quality about Christ's resurrected appearance that was different. His body was changed enough for Mary and His disciples to fail to recognize Him at first glance. However, after being with Him for a little while or hearing His voice or

observing His actions, those who had known Him recognized who He was, the risen Savior.

As Jesus' body was changed, so shall ours be. Since our bodies will be like His, we shall have bodies of flesh and bone that are incorruptible, will never wear out, decay or die. Our resurrected bodies will never again experience pain. And our real, spiritual bodies will be able to transcend space and time. Jesus was able to enter locked rooms and disappear quickly from one place only to appear in another (Matthew 28:10; Mark 16:11-12; Luke 24:31). In our resurrected bodies we, too, will have this supernatural control over matter.[1]

Our Resurrection Minds

To this, Grant Jeffrey says:

In the same way that our resurrected bodies will resemble Christ's, our minds and emotions and personalities will also be affected by this new reality. The Bible clearly shows that after His resurrection, Jesus retained His love for His disciples, His concern for the welfare of His followers and an interest in their feelings. In our resurrection bodies we, too, will still feel the same love for our friends and families. We will experience a rich emotional life full of joy, peace, love and thanksgiving. Though Jesus said that marriage would not exist in heaven, "For in the resurrection they neither marry, nor are given in marriage, but are as the angels of God in heaven" (Matthew 22:30), the spiritual essence of a pure, holy love will find its highest expression in an eternal cherishing of our loved ones.

Many assume that once we obtain our resurrection bodies and enter heaven we will automatically become bland, neutral saints without distinctive features of personality. This assumption is far from the truth given to us by God. In eternity we shall manifest the perfected form of the character we are building today. Christ will remove the sin in our lives, but we will still have those characteristics that make us unique as individuals. This diversity of personalities will provide one of the great joys of our future life and will make us recognizable to one another.

Others have expressed the fear that once they have acquired their resurrection bodies and are residents of heaven they will not be able to enjoy the activities that they enjoy on earth. They are afraid that they will lose all knowledge and awareness of earthly relationships and interests. Why should we? Heaven is a place we will enjoy. Our creative talents will most probably flourish, and we will know and understand the vast secrets of our universe. We will be able to satisfy our curiosity about creation, history or science, and we will finally understand why certain things happened as they did. We will have greater vision and awareness because our current barriers of time and space will no longer limit us. In heaven we shall use all the faculties and gifts that our Creator has given us. And we shall do so to give Him glory.[2]

The Transportation of the Tribulation Survivors

Back in Matthew 22:10, we read that the king's servants invited all the people they could find—"both good and bad, and the wedding hall was filled with guests." How will these people get to Jerusalem? We may have our answer in Isaiah 49:20-22:

"The children born during your bereavement will yet say in your hearing, 'This place is too small for us; give us more space to live in.' Then you will say in your heart, 'Who bore me these? I was bereaved and barren; I was exiled and rejected. Who brought these up? I was left all alone, but these—where have they come from?'" This is what the Sovereign LORD says: "See, I will beckon to the Gentiles, I will lift up my banner to the peoples; they will bring your sons in their arms and carry your daughters on their shoulders."

We want to be careful not to read something into a passage that doesn't fit with Scripture. But this prophetic passage in Isaiah seems to say that those in exile—those rejected, those left all alone—will be startled to see the friendly face of a Gentile who was sent by the Lord to deliver them from their predicament.

It might be that the first work of the returning bride of Christ in the millennium will be to go to every corner of the globe and search every cave, hamlet, hut, and underground bunker, and find the survivors of the Tribulation period, both good and bad, both Jews and Gentiles, and somehow bring them to Jerusalem.

Future Story: Gerald Is Found

It had been nearly seven years since Gerald's wife, Ruth, and his two children had been taken up in the rapture. For the last three-and-a-half years he had led an underground movement using "the fishnet" to reach the seekers with the gospel, but recently even that had become difficult and now life was just a matter of survival. Months of malnutrition had laid waste to his once-200-pound frame, which was now 140 pounds of flesh and bones. Exposure to the cold weather with little shelter and the complete absence of any medical attention had greatly weakened Gerald's immune system. Infection ravaged his body, and his physical condition had deteriorated significantly. His clothes were torn and ragged, as were the blankets and moth-eaten mattress that made up his bed at night. Water was scarce, which affected Gerald's health even more.

One night, Gerald tried to pull himself to his feet and felt so sick and weak he knew that unless something changed, he wouldn't live much longer. His only reason for staying alive was the blessed hope he found in the Bible, which promised that Messiah would come back and set up a kingdom that would never end. But would it happen in the brief time that he had left on this earth? And what about his wife, Ruth? Where was she, and what was she doing? Opening up the tattered Bible that had been his guidepost during the Tribulation years, Gerald turned to Revelation. Tears came to his eyes as he read this in the diminishing light:

> I saw heaven standing open and there before me was a white horse, whose rider is called Faithful and True. With justice he judges and makes war. His eyes are like blazing fire, and on his head are many crowns. He has a name written on him that no one knows but he himself. He is dressed in a robe dipped in blood, and his name is the Word of God. The armies of heaven were following him, riding on white horses and dressed in fine linen, white and clean. Out of his mouth comes a sharp sword with which to strike down the nations. "He will rule

them with an iron scepter." He treads the winepress of the fury of the wrath of God Almighty. On his robe and on his thigh he has this name written: King of kings and Lord of lords (Revelation 19:11-16).

If only my King would come tonight and get me out of this hell on earth, thought Gerald as the memories of the horrors and deaths of recent months caused a wave of nausea to overcome him. Gerald collapsed on the mattress into a deep sleep.

Then Gerald felt his body being lifted from the mattress as he drifted between consciousness and reality. These were gentle hands holding him, unlike the hurting hands of the gangs that had roamed the cities at night. A sudden burst of energy coursed through his body as he opened his eyes and saw a beautiful woman before him. Her flawless skin glowed with radiance, her hair was like silk, and the white linen robe she wore was exquisitely tailored for her. "Ruth, is that you?"

"Yes Jerry, it's me," came the gentle reply that had been so characteristic of the woman he had married.

"But Ruth, where have you been? and how did you find me?"

"Gerald, you were never alone. God has been your protector these last seven years, since the day you became a believer. I have been sent by Messiah to bring you to Jerusalem for a banquet. Jehovah has prepared it especially for you."

Together they rose to begin their journey to Jerusalem.

The Coming Judgment

At the wedding feast, we see what happens next:

When the king came in to see the guests, he noticed a man there who was not wearing wedding clothes. "Friend," he asked, "how did you get in here without wedding clothes?" The man was speechless. "Then the king told the attendants, 'Tie him hand and foot, and throw him outside, into the darkness, where there will be weeping and gnashing of teeth.'" For many are invited, but few are chosen.

After the Tribulation, all the survivors left on earth will somehow be transported to Jerusalem to stand before Jesus. In Matthew 25 these people are likened to sheep and goats, with the sheep belonging to Jesus and the goats belonging to Satan:

When the Son of man comes in his glory, and all the angels with him, he will sit on his throne in heavenly glory: All the nations will be gathered before him, and he will separate the people one from another as a shepherd separates the sheep from the goats. He will put the sheep on his right and the goats on the left....

Then the King will say to those on his right, "Come, you who are blessed by my Father, take your inheritance, the kingdom prepared for you since the creation of the world: For I was hungry, and you gave me something to eat, I was thirsty and you gave me something to drink, I was a stranger, and you invited me in, I needed clothes and you clothed me, I was sick and you looked after me, I was in prison and you came to visit me."

Then the righteous will answer him, "Lord, when did we see you hungry and feed you, or thirsty, and gave you something to drink? When did we see you a stranger, and invite you in, or needing clothes and clothe you? When did we see you sick or in prison and go to visit you?" The King will reply, "I tell you the truth, whatever you did for one of the least of these brothers of mine, you did for me" (verses 31; 34-40).

In this passage we are confronted with a group of people—Christians—who had been living under terrible conditions. Many had been imprisoned or barely surviving with meager rations of food and water, unable to buy or sell or hold a job because of their faith in Jesus. They were willing to suffer for Jesus rather than take the mark of the beast. Their bodies were emaciated from food and sleep depravation. One by one they came to Jesus and bowed before the throne. A man, blind from birth, walked up to Jesus. Jesus had compassion on him and touched his eyes, and immediately the man could see the incredible things that God had in store for the millennium saints. Next, a man with a withered hand came up. Jesus said, "Stretch forth your hand," and the hand was restored whole. One by one the people came to Jesus, and all were made whole. Free of disease, suffering, and pain, they will now live for 1,000 years in the millennial kingdom, and then forever in the eternal kingdom.

What about those who don't receive Christ as Savior? We read about them next:

> Then he will say to those on his left, "Depart from me, you who are cursed, into the eternal fire prepared for the devil and his angels: For I was hungry and you gave me nothing to eat, I was thirsty and you gave me nothing to drink, I was a stranger and you did not invite me in, I needed clothes and you did not clothe me, I was sick and in prison and you did not look after me." They also will answer, "Lord, when did we see you hungry or thirsty or a stranger or needing clothes or sick or in prison, and did not help you?" He will reply, "I tell you the

truth, whatever you did not do for one of the least
of these, you did not do for me." Then they will go
away to eternal punishment, but the righteous to
eternal life (Matthew 25:41-46).

These people lived under the Antichrist's regime for
seven years. They had accepted the mark of identification
that enabled them to live comfortably and participate in the
global government. Some of these people might have been
sympathetic to the tribulation Christians, but their alignment with the Antichrist's kingdom sealed their ultimate
fate. They, like the sheep, will be brought before the new
King, who will mete out their judgment. They will suffer
punishment in hell, and later, everlasting punishment in the
lake of fire, which was prepared for the devil and his angels.

The great prophet, Daniel, had a vision that offers us a
picture of what this judgment might look like:

> As I looked, thrones were set in place, and the
> Ancient of Days took his seat. His clothing was as
> white as snow; the hair of his head was white like
> wool. His throne was flaming with fire, and its
> wheels were all ablaze. A river of fire was flowing,
> coming out from before him. Thousands upon thou-
> sands attended him; ten thousand times ten thou-
> sand stood before him. The court was seated, and the
> books were opened. Then I continued to watch
> because of the boastful words the horn [the Anti-
> christ] was speaking. I kept looking until the beast
> was slain and its body destroyed and thrown into the
> blazing fire....
>
> In my vision at night I looked, and there before me
> was one like a son of man, coming with the clouds of
> heaven. He approached the Ancient of Days and was
> led into his presence. He was given authority, glory
> and sovereign power; all peoples, nations and men of

every language worshiped him. His dominion is an everlasting dominion that will not pass away, and his kingdom is one that will never be destroyed.

I, Daniel, was troubled in spirit, and the visions that passed through my mind disturbed me. I approached one of those standing there and asked him the true meaning of all this. So he told me and gave me the interpretation of these things...the saints of the Most High will receive the kingdom and will possess it forever—yes, for ever and ever (Daniel 7:9-18).

It is no wonder that Daniel was troubled in spirit—he was witnessing the destruction of Satan's kingdom. God's ultimate purpose for this earth, which was cut off when Adam and Eve sinned, is to bring everything under His subjection through man. Since the fall of man, Satan's world powers have tried to imitate this world dominance and every attempt has failed and will continue to fail. Satan is a false king. God alone has the authority and the power to bring all things into subjection to Himself.

The fulfillment of Daniel's prophecy and of numerous other prophecies related to the coming millennial kingdom is a biblical and theological necessity. If there is no kingdom, with Christ as the literal reigning king, then God's purpose for man and His purpose for earth and the universe would never be brought to fruition. Satan's kingdom would be victorious over God's.

A Kingdom of Believers

At the beginning of the millennial kingdom, for the first time since the flood, the earth will be wholly populated by believers. These believers will enter into a new era of peace and utopia such as the world has never known since the Garden of Eden. Those believers will be comprised of both Jews and Gentiles. Those who survive the Tribulation will go into that kingdom in their natural bodies, and will have children and start populating the millennial kingdom. Those who came down from heaven with Christ will have glorified bodies.

Utopia on Earth

Author and prophecy expert Tim LaHaye says this about the coming kingdom:

> If the story of this incredible utopian kingdom age God has planned for mankind were better known by this world, I believe millions more would want to learn about salvation. Particularly if we were to compare God's incredibly great plans for His children with any other religious teaching or philosophical concept in the world—nothing else even comes close! How could reincarnation, soul sleep, purgatory, "the happy hunting grounds" or any other man-made doctrine of life in the afterlife compare with the wonderful plan God details in the Bible for our future?
>
> Unfortunately, this incredible plan is one of the best-kept secrets in the world. That must be part of the deception of Satan, to keep people from being inspired by the prophetic plan of God for their future. But whether known or unknown, it is going to come to pass, for it is guaranteed by the Word of the Lord; for the same prophet of God (Daniel) who interpreted that most important description of world empires from 606 B.C. to the end times has guaranteed the return of Jesus the Messiah to this earth to set up His kingdom. Why have there only been four world empires since the days of Nebuchadnezzar and his Babylonians (Medo-Persia, Greece, and Rome)? Because God, through His prophet Daniel, said that is all there would be! Genghis Khan tried to

conquer the world and failed, as did Napoleon, Kaiser Wilhelm, Adolf Hitler, Josef Stalin, Mao Tse-tung, and others. They never succeeded—and won't until "the man of sin" comes on the scene and becomes king over ten kings, after which Christ, the stone cut out of the mountain without hands, will grind the kingdoms of the world to powder and His kingdom will fill the whole earth.[3]

In those closing words, Tim LaHaye was referring to the prophecy described in Daniel 2:44-47, where we see Daniel speaking to King Nebuchadnezzar:

In the time of those kings, the God of heaven will set up a kingdom that will never be destroyed, nor will it be left to another people. It will crush all those kingdoms and bring them to an end, but it will itself endure forever. This is the meaning of the vision of the rock cut out of a mountain, but not by human hands—a rock that broke the iron, the bronze, the clay, the silver and the gold to pieces. The great God has shown the king what will take place in the future. The dream is true and the interpretation is trustworthy.

Then King Nebuchadnezzar fell prostrate before Daniel and paid him honor and ordered that an offering and incense be presented to him. The king said to Daniel, "Surely your God is the God of gods and the Lord of kings and a revealer of mysteries, for you were able to reveal this mystery."

The blessings God will rain upon this earth during Christ's millennial kingdom are beyond human comprehension. Can you even imagine a time so blessed of God that the best word you can think of to define it is *utopia*? It will literally be a taste of heaven on earth. As we shall see, it will be a time of righteousness, for Christ will reign over the whole earth. It will be a time of unprecedented material blessing; the prophets tell us that the reapers will follow the sowers. And there will be no more war, for in that day people will "beat their swords into plowshares" (see Isaiah 2:4).

The Temples—Past and Future

In the millennial kingdom, the first order from King Jesus will be to rebuild the Temple. God's plan for His Temple was first revealed to Moses at the foot of Mount Sinai: "Have them make a sanctuary for me, and I will dwell among them" (Exodus 25:8). This was the Tabernacle, a movable structure that would serve as God's dwelling place for 485 years. Later God would have Solomon build a permanent structure. His charge to the people of Israel concerning the preparations for the First Temple included this: "The task is great, because this palatial structure is not for man but for the LORD God" (1 Chronicles 29:1). But why did God need a place where He could dwell among His people?

The First Temple

After God delivered the children of Israel from the hand of Pharaoh, He led them into the Sinai Desert to the foot of Mount Sinai. They would remain there for almost a year. The mountain was cordoned off to prevent the children of Israel from touching the mountain and being consumed by the presence of God. Moses wrote, "The mountain blazed with fire to the very heavens, with black clouds and deep darkness" (Deuteronomy 4:11). God's descent was accompanied by smoke, fire, thunder caused by lightning, trumpet sounds, and a great earthquake. This awesome display of heavenly power caused terror to spread throughout the camp. The people cried to Moses to keep God from speaking to them lest they die. Moses told them not to worry; God just wanted to move from the mountain into the camp. That was just what the people needed to hear! This was the God who destroyed the land of Egypt by plagues and drowned the mighty Egyptian army in the Red Sea. And now He was on this mountain that was consumed by fire and smoke, warning the people not to approach His presence or die. This God was going to camp with them! Great fear came over the children of Israel.

This fear came from the knowledge that God and man could not co-exist together. In the Garden of Eden, God was able to walk with and commune with Adam and Eve in their original sinless state. But when Adam and Eve sinned, a barrier was set up between God and man. Sinful man could no longer go to God and see Him face to face because he would be consumed by God's holy presence.

The fall of man did not take God by surprise. Nor did it deter God from wanting to restore His relationship with man. God eventually made this possible through the work of Jesus Christ. But in those days when Israel was in the wilderness, God chose for the Tabernacle to be His dwelling place, a holy place that would keep Israel from being consumed. This dwelling place was modeled after God's heavenly Temple, and God gave Moses the blueprints containing instructions for building His dwelling place on earth.

What the people of Israel could not comprehend was that the Tabernacle represented a pivotal point in Israel's history. God was returning to Israel, there in the Sinai, what had been lost in Eden: a personal relationship through His presence.

The Tabernacle was used for 485 years, serving as a temporary structure that was moved from place to place. When King David conquered Jebusite Jerusalem and made it the capital of Israel, the time had come to build a permanent structure for God. After the Temple was built, the Tabernacle was incorporated into it, establishing continuity between the two structures.

Solomon, David's son, built the first Temple in 960 B.C. God's design was for His blessings to flow from this Temple in Jerusalem and spread through the whole earth. It stood for nearly 400 years on a hill overlooking Jerusalem. Then in 587 B.C., the Babylonian army burned down the Temple, along with the palace complex and all the houses of the city. The ruins would remain untouched for the next 70 years while the Israelites lived in captivity in Babylon.

The Second Temple

Zerubbabel's Temple

At the end of the 70-year exile, under the leadership of Zerubbabel, about 50,000 Jews returned to Jerusalem in 538 B.C. and began to lay the foundation for the Second Temple. The work was finally completed 20 years later, after a decree from the Persian king Darius not only permitted the rebuilding but also prescribed that local taxes be paid to the Jews to help finance the construction. For the next 200 years, the Second Temple served as the official center of worship for the children of Israel.

Author and Middle Eastern expert Dr. Randall Price, in his book, *The Coming Last Days Temple,* explains what happened next:

> During this period, Judea came under the control of the Greeks through Alexander the Great and later his generals Ptolemy and Seleucis, yielding the Egyptian Greeks (Ptolemies) and the Syrian Greeks (Seleucids). Alexander and Ptolemy treated the Jews favorably and allowed continued governorship by the high priests, but during the reign of the Syrian Greek ruler Antiochus IV Epiphanes (175–164

B.C.), strife broke out. As a result, two Jewish factions, Orthodox and Hellenist (Jews who adopted Greek culture), contended for the high priesthood. Antiochus IV naturally sided with the Hellenistic party, and appointed a high priest who permitted pagan worship. The events surrounding this man's successor brought an invasion of Jerusalem in 170 B.C., in which many Jews were killed and the Temple—along with its restored treasures—was plundered. Antiochus further desecrated the Temple by sacrificing an unclean animal (a pig) on the Temple altar and by erecting a statue of Zeus Olympias in the Holy of Holies in 168 B.C. This action had been predicted by the prophet Daniel (Daniel 8:23-25; 11:21-35) and served as a partial fulfillment of the type of desecration the Temple would one day suffer under the Antichrist.[4]

Finally, in December 164 B.C., Judas Maccabeas liberated Jerusalem, purified the Temple, and reinstituted the daily offerings. That day has been celebrated ever since as Hanukkah, or the Feast of Dedication.

The Temple was desecrated again in the year 63 B.C. when the Roman general Pompey entered Jerusalem. Thousands of Jews threw themselves on the ground and begged him not to enter the Temple and desecrate the Holy Place. Pompey was convinced that the Temple must contain great riches and hidden secrets, so he entered the Holy Place and even marched into the Holy of Holies. He found no statues or symbols representing God. Tradition says that when he emerged he looked around at the Jews in wonder and said, "It is empty; there is nothing there but darkness." He ordered the city to be torn down, but he left the Temple intact, and the people of Israel were now under Roman rule.

Herod's Temple

In 37 B.C., Rome placed a ruler named Herod over the Jews. Under his dynasty, Herod proposed the rebuilding of the Temple of Zerubbabel, which was now in a state of disrepair. Herod's plans included the complete demolition of the Temple and a new one to be rebuilt at the same site. The actual Temple took seven years to complete, but extensive detail work on the Temple complex continued for the next 75 years.

It was in this Temple that the baby Jesus was taken to be dedicated to the Lord, in accord with the law that stated, "Every firstborn male is to be consecrated to the Lord" (Luke 2:23). Then some 12 years later, Jesus returned to the Temple for his Jewish *mitzvot*, during which He made an interesting statement.

Jesus and the Temple

After the days of the Passover feast were completed, Mary and Joseph began their journey back home with a group of other people, but Jesus stayed in Jerusalem. Mary and Joseph, unaware of this, actually traveled a full day's journey into the desert before they discovered that Jesus was missing. Upon returning to Jerusalem, it took them three days to find Jesus. He had spent those three days in the Temple debating the teachers, who were astonished at His understanding and wisdom. When Mary and Joseph saw Jesus, Mary scolded Jesus for causing them sorrow. Jesus' answer to His parents shows His relationship to the Temple: "Why were you searching for me? Didn't you know I had to be in my Father's house?" (Luke 2:49). These are the first recorded words of Jesus in Scripture. If we take them to mean that the Temple was a place where Jesus "had to be," a place that He identified as His "Father's house," then we can understand why the first thing on Jesus' agenda when He returns to earth will be to rebuild the Temple.

The Second Temple Is Destroyed

Just before His famous Olivet discourse, Jesus made a proclamation against Jerusalem and specifically the Temple: "O Jerusalem, Jerusalem, thou that killest the prophets, and stonest them which are sent unto thee, how often would I have gathered thy children together, even as a hen gathered her chickens under her wings, and ye would not! Behold, your house is left unto you desolate" (Matthew 23:37-38 KJV). The context of those words makes it clear that the Temple is the focal point of Jesus' statement. Jesus then "went out, and departed from the temple: and his disciples came to him for to show him the buildings of the temple. And Jesus said unto them, See ye not all these things? Verily I say unto you, There shall not be left here one stone upon another, that shall not be thrown down" (Matthew 24:1-2). Sure enough, the Romans destroyed the city of Jerusalem and the Temple in A.D. 70.

The Tribulation Temple

Since A.D. 70, the Temple Mount has not been the home of a Jewish Temple. Yet we know that eventually, another Temple will be built. In the Bible, we are told that at the mid-point of the Tribulation period, the Antichrist will break his treaty with Israel and desecrate the Holy of Holies in the Temple (see Mark 13:14). Obviously there can be no abomination of desolation without a Temple. Also, some Jews believe it's necessary to build the Temple in order to obey the standing command by Jehovah to "make a sanctuary for me" (Exodus 25:8). With the pact in place between Israel and the Antichrist at the beginning of the Tribulation period, the Jews would not have to accept the Antichrist as their Messiah in order to build the Temple. On the other hand, it is possible that those who build the Temple will be deceived into thinking that the covenant made with the Antichrist will have ushered in the everlasting Messianic era. It will be a rude awakening for these Jews to see their Temple desecrated.

The Millennial Temple

After the Tribulation Temple comes the Millennial Temple. A full description of this Temple and its courts is given in Ezekiel 40:1–44:31. No such building as Ezekiel so minutely describes has ever yet been built, and so the prophecy cannot refer to either Zerubbabel's or Herod's Temple, and because there is to be no Temple in the New Jerusalem, it must be a description of the Temple that is to be on the earth during the millennium. That it does not belong to the new earth is also clear, for the land in which it is located is bound by the sea, and the waters that flow from it flow "into the sea," but in the new earth there is "no more sea" (Revelation 21:1). This is still further confirmed by Ezekiel's mention of the desert, the Jordan River, the Mediterranean Sea, and other localities that will not be found on the new earth after its renovation by fire.

The Aaronic Priesthood will be reestablished, and the sons of Zadok shall officiate and offer sacrifices (Ezekiel 44:15-31). The new Temple, however, will lack many things that were a part of the old Temple. There will be no Ark of the Covenant, no pot of manna, no Aaron's rod, no Tables of the Law, no cherubim, no mercy seat, no golden candlestick, no shew bread, no Altar of Incense, no veil, no unapproachable Holy of Holies where the high priest alone might enter, nor is there any high priest to offer atonement for sin or to make intercession for the people, unless a rather obscure passage in Zechariah 6:12-13 means that Christ (the Branch of

Jeremiah 23:5-6) shall be a "King-Priest" and perform the duties of high priest conjointly with His kingly office.

While the Levites as a class will perform the Temple service, they will be barred from priestly duties because of their past sins (Ezekiel 44:10-14). There will be a daily morning sacrifice, but no evening sacrifice (Ezekiel 46:13-15). They will present the burnt offering, grain offering, drink offering, sin offering, and fellowship offering (Ezekiel 45:17), and the guilt offering (Ezekiel 42:13). Two feasts are to be observed: the Passover, but no Passover lamb will be offered as Jesus was the final Passover lamb (Ezekiel 45:21-24), and the Feast of Tabernacles (Zechariah 14:16-19). All the nations will be required to observe this feast under penalty of drought or plague.

The Feast of Pentecost will be done away with on account of its fulfillment. The Day of Pentecost, recorded in Acts 2:1-4, was only a partial fulfillment of the prophecy of Joel 2:28-32. No such wonders in the heavens and the earth as blood, fire, pillars of smoke, the "sun…turned to darkness," and the "moon [turning] to blood" occurred at Pentecost. But all those things will happen before "the great and dreadful day of the Lord" (Joel 2:31).

The conversion of the Jewish nation will be sealed with a great outpouring of the Holy Spirit. Whether this shall be universal or only upon Israel is not clear. The original prophecy in Joel was given to Israel, and its partial fulfillment at Pentecost seems to have been limited to that nation. The knowledge of the Lord, however, will be worldwide, and "it shall come to pass, that ten men…of all languages of the nations, even shall take hold of the skirt of him that is a Jew, saying, 'We will go with you: for we have heard that God is with you'" (Zechariah 8:22-23). There will be one "universal religion" in that day (Malachi 1:11). The "Shekinah glory" that departed from the Temple at the time of the

Babylonian captivity (Ezekiel 10:18-20; 11:22-23) will again take up its residence in the new Temple (Ezekiel 43:1-5).[5] The whole earth will be filled with the blessings of God flowing from the Temple. What a world that will be!

Will King Jesus Use Leading-edge Technology?

There is no reason to believe that this world will go back to a time when there was no exponential technology growth. For the first few years of the millennium, with everyone a believer, technology will be used only for good. The conditions of this earth will be conducive for an explosion in technology the likes of which we can't even imagine now. The five great technowaves—the computer wave, the global communications wave, the biotech wave, the nanotechnology wave, and the alternative energy wave—all begun in premillennial times, will once again begin to flourish. But this time, there will be one new factor that affects the growth and convergence of these great waves. The King of the universe, whose residence is now at Millennial Palace, Jerusalem, will direct the world's greatest physicists, scientists, doctors, engineers, teachers, and laborers in developing these technologies for the good of mankind and the universe. Man's thinking will change. Companies that were once national and international in their vision will now become universal in scope. The galaxies will be within the reach of this millennial kingdom.

Global Communication During the Millennial Reign

In the new global economy, will there be high-tech telecommunications? We believe so. Most likely the world will enter a time of universal connection. The millennial Internet originating from Millennial Palace in Jerusalem will be light years different from what passes for today's Internet. The following four elements will probably define the millennial Internet, over which information could eventually travel at the speed of thought.

1. *Multimedia webcasting*: Publishing in the millennial reign of Christ will be targeted, with interactive content able to be directed to one person or to millions through computers, television, appliances, phones, and any number of other media channels that today are mostly one-way.

2. *Personalized content*: The information sent will be able to be customized based on a sophisticated real-time relationship with the individual or group. It may happen like this:

> The individual engages the online agent, and, during the interacting, the online agent will "learn" in real time how best to meet the needs of the individual. The online site then transforms itself into a content and interactive form that may appeal to the individual. The online site then intelligently communicates and interacts, building a rapport and kind of bonding to the individual. It might be that intuitive intelligence will be built into websites that serve individuals or millions automatically and concurrently. This intuitive intelligence will make everyone feel important.

3. *Personalized purchases*: Another possible aspect of this new information highway is intuitive transaction agents, possibly voice or video personalities, that will get to know and even discover what an individual wants and will help to find it at the right place or price.

4. *Personalized Internet communities*: Net communities could be established that allow people of like interests to engage in virtual experiences online. There will still be people who enjoy fly-fishing, those who like to ski the slopes, those who like to bowl, and yes, those who like to work with computers (after all, who is going to put this incredible knowledge experience together?). Site visitors will be able to "walk" through shops, trying out the newest fly-rod in a clear Canadian stream filled with record-size trout, or test a new pair of skis on a world-class slope high in the Swiss Alps. The virtual experience will include emotions, sensory information, digital touch, and smell. You might even be able to fish or ski alongside an individual who is experiencing the same virtual environment as you but is thousands of miles away. This social computing will bring the world together into one large global community.

Millennial Reign: Year Three

A gentle ring woke Gerald Litman. His eyes opened to see a wall-sized screen depicting the Temple in Jerusalem, just ten miles from his apartment. A slow moving waterway, lined with exotic trees, proceeded out of the Temple, passed through the priests' portion and into the outer court, and continued through the countryside until it emptied into the Living Sea, once called the Dead Sea.

This day, as always, there were worship songs emanating from the outer court as the Temple singers offered their songs of praise to King Jesus. Billions of people were watching with Gerald as Jesus entered the court and addressed the world. At the conclusion of the address, a warm, friendly face Gerald had named Holly, replaced the Temple scene, cheerily announcing, "Gerald, it's time to get out of bed and start your day."

Gerald jumped out of bed. His 200-pound frame hit the floor hands first, and he did 100 pushups and 100 sit-ups. "Not bad," he said to himself, "for a man who, just a few years ago, was near death." Gerald remembered once again that day when he bowed in the presence of his Messiah, King Jesus, and said, "I am not worthy to have a part in your kingdom." Jesus, however, assured him by saying, "I tell you the truth, whatever you did for one of the least of these brothers of mine, you did for Me." Then, the most amazing thing had happened: Jesus had touched Gerald's body and said, "You are now made clean. I am giving you a body that will never get sick and will never wear out. You used 'the fishnet' to communicate to believers around the globe; now I want you to direct the new Global Spiritual Brain and set up links in every corner of the world. No one should be without a direct link to the Temple in Jerusalem."

Since then, Gerald had completed his Ph.D. in religion and theology at the Millennial Institute in Jerusalem. His dissertation was titled, "Reaching the World Through the Global Spiritual Brain," and Gerald was looking forward to starting his new assignment from Jesus.

Walking into his kitchen, the appliances sensed Gerald's presence. The coffeepot turned itself on. Bread was toasted to the setting he preferred. His favorite worship music gently filled the air. The intelligent house was now coming to life.

On the coffee table, Holly had prepared Gerald's personalized edition of the *Jerusalem Universe* newspaper by scanning the Global Spiritual Brain (once called the Internet). The newspaper-sized sheet of digital paper changed as he touched the corner. The headline read, "World Renewal Project on Track to Finish in Millennial Reign (MR) 10."

Living in the Millennial Kingdom

The failed attempt at a global religion during the reign of Antichrist will stand in sharp contrast to the successful one-world religion under the reign of King Jesus.

With God's presence among people, the world's climate will be conducive for people to become Christians. What's more, "never again will there be...in it an infant who lives but a few days, or an old man who does not live out his years; he who dies at a hundred will be thought a mere youth; he who fails to reach a hundred will be considered accursed" (Isaiah 65:20). This verse points out that there will no longer be infant mortality in the millennium, for everyone born during this time will reach a certain age. The verse also says that the person who dies at 100 years of age will be considered young. Everyone born in the millennium, then, will live at least 100 years. Those who die at the age of 100 years will be sinners or unbelievers in Christ because they "will be considered accursed." So death in the millennial kingdom will only be for unbelievers.

As was already stated, at the beginning of Christ's millennial reign, there will be many Jewish and Gentile believers who were Tribulation survivors. They will still have their natural bodies and be able to bear children. The children of these Tribulation survivors will need salvation, for they will have inherited their parents' sin nature, which goes back to the fall of Adam and Eve in the Garden.

In Matthew 28:18-20, Jesus gave the mandate to take the gospel to all the nations, and He said that this commission would continue to the very end of the age. That mandate does not end with the victory of Christ at the end of the Tribulation period. As the Bible says, the world will have 1,000 years to prepare for one more battle between King Jesus and Satan:

> When the thousand years are over, Satan will be released from his prison and will go out to deceive the nations in the four corners of the earth—Gog and Magog—to gather them for battle. In number they are like the sand on the seashore. They marched across the breadth of the earth and surrounded the camp of God's people, the city he loves. But fire came down from heaven and devoured them (Revelation 20:7-9).

Only those who are believers will be prepared for this battle. Those who are born during the millennial kingdom will have at least 100 years to accept Christ as their personal Lord and Savior, according to Isaiah. And those who do receive Christ will survive this final battle and go on to eternity, which will be inhabited by the new heaven and the new earth. Thus, we who are Christians will be called to continue proclaiming the gospel message all through the millennium, taking it to all four corners of the earth:

Then the survivors from all the nations that have attacked Jerusalem will go up year after year to worship the King, the LORD Almighty, and to celebrate the Feast of Tabernacles. If any of the peoples of the earth do not go up to Jerusalem to worship the King, the LORD Almighty, they will have no rain. If the Egyptian people do not go up and take part, they will have no rain. The LORD will bring on them the plague he inflicts on the nations that do not go up to celebrate the Feast of Tabernacles. This will be the punishment of Egypt and the punishment of all the nations that do not go up to celebrate the Feast of Tabernacles (Zechariah 14:17-19).

Once a year, Jerusalem will be the center of attention.

Sunday at Millennium Church: MR 100

The congregation is suddenly hushed in reverence as the wall in front of them turns into a screen and Jesus, their Great Shepherd, delivers the sermon. Standing in regal splendor, at the Temple in Jerusalem, every word that comes from His mouth seems to speak to the need of every individual in the congregation. This message is also being received by billions of people across the world. His message is clear.

I am the Alpha and the Omega, the First and the Last, the Beginning and the End. Blessed are those who wash their robes, that they may have the right to the tree of life and may go through the gates into the city. Outside are the dogs, those who practice magic arts, the sexually immoral, the murderers, the idolaters and everyone who loves and practices falsehood. I, Jesus, have sent my angel to give you this testimony for the churches. I am the Root and the Offspring of David, and the bright Morning Star (Revelation 22:13-16).

The one common thread that links all the ages—from the Garden of Eden to the millennium—is that all men will be required to make a choice about God: whether to accept or reject His plan of salvation. Those who choose to receive Him will have a place in the millennial kingdom and the eternal new heavens and the new earth. Those who do not receive Him will die in their sins, be judged, and then sent to the eternal lake of fire.

The choice you make about receiving Jesus Christ is without a doubt the most important decision you will make on this earth. At this point, God is more interested in what you believe in your heart than what you say with your lips. Have you personally invited Jesus Christ into your life as Lord and Savior? If you haven't, then you are invited to do so right where you are. Just pray this prayer, believing it in your heart:

Lord Jesus, I now transfer my trust from myself and the things around me and I place it entirely in you. Forgive me for all my sins. I repent and turn away from my sins and want to follow you. Thank you for paying the penalty of sin on the cross that I can receive your gift of eternal life. Jesus, be the Lord and Savior of my life. In Jesus' name, amen.

If you have accepted Christ as your personal Lord and Savior, then not only will you have the joy of experiencing the millennial reign of Christ, but you will also live forever in eternity with Him—which is the topic of our next chapter.

15

Eternity: Beyond the Wave

The future is limitless. Beyond the Tribulation and the millennial kingdom lies the final reality: the eternal state. This is a powerful reminder that this present world is not the end. There is indeed a new world coming where God is in complete control. Even the blessings of the earthly millennium will not compare with the glorious eternity that awaits the children of God.

John the revelator was not the first to see all the way down the canyon of eternity. Isaiah the prophet also foresaw the new heavens and a new earth (Isaiah 65:17-25; 66:22-24). He even went so far as to say, "The former shall not be remembered, nor come into mind" (Isaiah 65:17 KJV). The apostle Peter, too, spoke of "new heavens and a new earth" (2 Peter 3:13 KJV). Peter said the present world is "reserved unto fire against the day of judgment" (3:7). He predicted a time when "the heavens shall pass away with a great noise, and the elements shall melt with fervent heat....Nevertheless we, according to his promise, look for new heavens and a new earth, wherein dwelleth righteousness" (2 Peter 3:10,13 KJV).

Revelation chapter 21 introduces us to a whole new series of events. We have entered the final phase of the apocalypse—eternity. All judgments are now concluded. God will wipe away all the tears from our eyes, and there will be no more sorrow nor death. Even with all the blessings of the millennium, human sufferings were not totally eliminated. But in God's new world order, they are no more. Wilbur Smith wrote: "In Revelation 21:1–22:5 we have the most extensive revelation of the eternal home of the redeemed to be found anywhere in the Scriptures, and most suitably it forms the conclusion of all the revelation of the ages recorded in our Bible. The remaining verses (Revelation 22:6-21) are simply an appendix including an exhortation, warning and promise."[1]

John begins his final vision with the familiar words, "And I saw" (Revelation 21:1), reminding us again that the entire book of Revelation is a vision of future events. As such, we need to keep in mind that what he saw was recorded in the vocabulary, language, and descriptive terms of his own time. What he actually means by "streets of gold" or "gates of pearl" may be beyond our wildest imagination or expectation. But that he sees a real place is obvious. He describes it as a city (Revelation 21:2), speaks of its inhabitants (verse 24), its gates (verse 12), its size (verse 16), its foundations (verse 14), and its walls (verse 18). He describes the eternal state as a place of great activity, worship, and service to God. He also speaks of it as our eternal home, where we shall dwell forever.

What's New in Eternity

In Revelation 21–22, it's interesting to note that John focuses on seven new things in the eternal state. While the number seven does not appear in these chapters, it is evident that the focus is on *seven "new" things* in the eternal state:

1. New heavens (21:1)

2. A new earth (21:1)

3. A new Jerusalem (21:2)

4. A new world order (21:5)

5. A new temple (21:22)

6. A new light (21:23)

7. A new paradise (22:1-5)

Here we find the redeemed of all time living in perfect peace and harmony in a final, fixed moral state in which there is no sin, no rebellion, no pain, no sorrow, nor death.

The terms "new heavens" and "new earth" indicate that a brand-new world is coming. "Heavens" (Greek, *ouranos*) refers to the atmospheric heavens (clouds, etc.), not to the dwelling place of God. That is, the old planet and its atmospheres will vanish and be replaced by a "new heavens and a new earth." The heaven where God dwells is often called the "third heaven" (see 2 Corinthians 12:2) and needs no replacement. It is the place from which the New Jerusalem descends to earth.

The New Jerusalem

The hopes and dreams of the Jewish prophets looked forward to a New Jerusalem (see Isaiah 60; Ezekiel 40–48). If we are correct in dating the writing of Revelation at circa A.D. 95, the old Jerusalem would already have been in ashes for about 25 years. Therefore, it should not surprise us that John anticipated the arrival of a brand-new city "coming down from God" out of the third heaven. This event is mentioned three times, in Revelation 3:12; 21; and 21:10.

The New Jerusalem is referred to as "a bride adorned for her husband" (21:2 KJV). Later (21:9-10), John makes it clear that this is the bride of the Lamb, who was first introduced in Revelation 19:7-16. She returned from heaven with Christ and ruled with Him during the millennial kingdom. Now she assumes a new and permanent position as the "holy city."

This time she is called both the "bride" and "wife" of the Lamb (21:9). Yet she is also referred to as a "city." Bible commentator Robert Thomas writes, "The figure of a bride-city captures two characteristics of the New Jerusalem: God's personal relationship with His people (i.e., the bride) and the life of the people in communion with Him (i.e., the city)."[2]

Bible scholar A.T. Robertson points out that "adorned" is from the Greek word from which we get the term *cosmetics*. The same term also applies to the adornment of the foundations of the city in Revelation 21:19-20.[3]

In anticipation of the bride's arrival, a "great voice" speaks from heaven announcing that the "tabernacle of God is with men" (Revelation 21:3). This is a most dramatic announcement. It indicates that God is now accessible to His people. He is no longer on the distant throne of heaven. Nor is He hidden beyond the veil in the Holy of Holies. Rather:

1. God will dwell with us.

2. We shall be His people.

3. He will be our God.

4. God will wipe away our tears.

5. There will be no more death.

6. There will be no more sorrow.

7. There will be no more pain.

Revelation 21:4 then declares, "For the former things are passed away." Then God Himself, the one on the throne, adds, "Behold, I make all things new" (verse 5). This one statement summarizes what the entire postscript is all about: "new things." This is not a repair job. Nor is it a major overhaul. It is a brand-new creation, and the new Jerusalem is the apex of that creation.

In addition to telling us what will be in heaven, John also lists *seven things* that will *not* be in the eternal state:

1. the sea (Revelation 21:1)

2. death (21:4)

3. mourning (21:4)

4. weeping (21:4)

5. pain (21:4)

6. the curse (22:3)

7. night (21:25)

Some have questioned the absence of the sea, but we must remember it was from the sea that the beast appeared in Revelation 13:1. Also, the absence of the sea indicates the eternal city is quite different from the natural world that now exists.

The picture painted in Revelation 21 is that of the new Jerusalem suspended between heaven and earth. It is the final and permanent bond between the two. Notice also that the new earth, not just heaven, is a part of the final state. It also appears that the redeemed saints of God will be able to travel from heaven to earth by means of the various levels of the eternal city.

The promise of God to believers is that those who overcome (or persevere) will "inherit all things" (Revelation 21:7). This is the only reference to the believer's spiritual and eternal inheritance in the book of Revelation. But the concept is mentioned frequently in the New Testament, especially by Jesus and Paul (see Matthew 5:5; 19:29; 25:34; Romans 4:13; 1 Corinthians 6:9). "All things" refers to all that is really essential and worthwhile for eternity. It is not a promise for earthly wealth and prosperity but for heavenly and eternal blessings. Paul had the same thing in mind when he wrote, "We know that all things work together for good to them that love God....He that spared not his own Son, but delivered him up for us all, how shall he not with him also freely give us all things?" (Romans 8:28,32 KJV).

By contrast, the ungodly, unrepentant, and unbelieving multitudes, introduced by the adversative "but," will never see the new Jerusalem. They will be cast into the lake of fire, which burns with fire and brimstone and is the "second death" (Revelation 21:8). There is no hope of a second chance mentioned. John describes these unbelievers in eight categories:

1. fearful

2. unbelieving

3. abominable

4. murderers

5. whoremongers

6. sorcerers

7. idolaters

8. liars

This is not to say that those who have ever committed these sins cannot be saved, but that those who continue to do so give evidence of an unrepentant and unconverted heart.

The Holy City

John was carried away "in the spirit" to a high mountain and shown the bride of Christ—the holy city of God. Beasley-Murray notes that "the Revelation as a whole may be characterized as A Tale of Two Cities, with the subtitle, 'The Harlot and the Bride.'"[4] With the collapse of Babylon, "the great harlot" (city of man), we were ushered into the millennium, where Christ will rule in the earthly Jerusalem. Now we see the ultimate: the city of God, the bride of the lamb, in all her eternal splendor and glory.

The most dominant characteristic of the holy city is the presence of the glory of God (Revelation 21:11). In the Old Testament, the *Shekinah* glory rested on the ark of the covenant in the Holy of Holies, but the prophet Ezekiel tells us that the glory departed before the final destruction of Solomon's Temple (see Ezekiel 8:4; 9:3; 10:4,18; 11:23). While the builders of the Second Temple prayed for the glory to return, there is no record that it ever did (Haggai 2:3). Israel's only hope in those dark days was that the glory would return one day (Haggai 2:7-9).

For more than 400 years, the Temple was dark and empty. It stood as a gaunt symbol of Israel's empty ritual—no glory, no God, no power. It was not until Christ was born and the angels appeared and the "glory of the Lord shone around them" that the glory returned (see Luke 2:9-14). The angels announced the birth of the Savior, Christ the Lord, and sang, "Glory to God in the highest." In the person of Jesus Christ, the glory had finally returned. However, Israel officially rejected the Messiah, and the glory was made available to Gentiles who by faith received the Savior and became the temples of the Holy Spirit (see 1 Corinthians 6:19-20). In the meantime, Jerusalem was destroyed, and the Second Temple with it, by the Romans in A.D. 70. And even when the Third Temple is built during the Tribulation, the glory will not return.

The glory of God will, however, be in full expression in the new Jerusalem (the "glory" symbolizes God's presence with His people). The fact that He is present is far more significant than the dazzling description of the city itself. John MacArthur makes this point when he asks whether there is a temple in heaven. He notes that Revelation 11:19 refers to "the temple of God which is in heaven" (NASB), whereas Revelation 21:22 says, "And I saw no temple in it, for the Lord God, the Almighty, and the Lamb are its temple" (NASB). Rejecting the idea that there is presently a temple in heaven that will be removed in the future, MacArthur writes, "The temple in heaven is not a building: it is the Lord God Almighty Himself....In other words, the glory of God both illuminates heaven and defines it as a temple. One might say all heaven is the temple, and the glory and presence of the Lord permeate it."[5]

The description of the city by John the revelator is as follows:

1. *Splendor:* like a jasper, clear as crystal (Revelation 21:11)

2. *Wall:* 144 cubits (220 feet) high (verse 17)

3. *Gates:* giant pearls, named for the 12 tribes of Israel (verses 12,21)

4. *Measurement:* foursquare—1,500-mile cube (verse 16)

5. *City itself:* pure gold, like clear glass (verse 18)

6. *Street:* pure gold, like transparent glass (verse 21)

7. *Temple:* God and the lamb are the temple (verse 22)

8. *Light:* glory of God and the lamb (verse 23)

9. *Nations:* those who are saved (verse 24)

10. *Access:* gates that are never closed (verse 25)

11. *Activity:* no night there (verse 25)

12. *Purity:* none who defile (verse 27)

A great deal has been written about whether this language is literal or symbolic or phenomenological. In truth, it combines all these elements. The whole book of Revelation is filled with symbolic language; therefore, we cannot overlook certain obvious symbols here: 12 gates, 12 foundations, foursquare. It is also obvious that John is attempting to describe the indescribable. Human language is not fully adequate to describe the glories of the heavenly city. Thus, we read of "transparent gold" and "gates of pearl."

What is clear is that John is describing a real place where the saved, and only the saved, will dwell with God forever. The unsaved are excluded from this city totally and completely. Satan and those he has deceived are all in the lake of fire, from which there is no escape. The reference to "nations" and "kings" should not surprise us; Jesus promised that the gospel would be preached unto all nations (Matthew 24:14). John has earlier introduced us to those in heaven as "a great multitude...from every nation" (Revelation 7:9). He has already referred to believers as "a kingdom and priests" who reign with Christ (Revelation 5:10).

The importance of our relationship to Christ is emphasized again in the last verse of the chapter (21:27). Only those whose names are written in the Lamb's book of life can live in the holy city. This includes all the redeemed of all time: the Old Testament saints, the New Testament saints, the Tribulation saints, and the millennial saints. In all these groups we will see the perfect blending of the redeemed in the holy city—the 12 gates are named for the 12 tribes of Israel, and the 12 foundations for the 12 apostles (who represent the New Testament believers). The final vision of biblical prophecy (Revelation 21–22) reveals all the redeemed in a state of eternal glory, reigning with Christ.

Paradise Regained

In the final chapter of Revelation, we learn that all that was lost in the beginning will finally be regained. Paradise is restored in the holy city. The biblical story, which began in the garden, ends in the eternal city. In between there stands the cross of Jesus Christ, which changed the destiny of mankind forever. Revelation 22 clearly indicates that the eternal state will return the new creation to the inherent qualities of the Garden of Eden, only on a grander scale. Then, and only then, will the Creator's true intention for humanity finally be realized.

The *river of life* is reminiscent of the river of Eden, whose tributaries flowed in four directions (Genesis 2:10,14). The metaphoric use of a river of spiritual refreshment can be found throughout the Old Testament (Psalm 36:9; Proverbs 10:11; 13:14; Isaiah 12:3; Jeremiah 2:13; 17:13; Ezekiel 47:9; Zechariah 14:8). The beautiful picture that is painted in Revelation 22 tells us that the best of the natural world will be preserved in the eternal world.

The *tree of life* is presented in Genesis 2:9 as a single tree. In Ezekiel's millennial vision, several trees are seen on both sides of the great river (Ezekiel 47:12). But the Revelation record reconnects us with the Genesis record: In both accounts, this tree is a singular tree. And here, in Revelation 22:2, it bears 12 types of fruit—one for each month of the year. Thus, it is perpetually in bloom. There is no winter season in the eternal state.

Revelation 22:2 says that "the leaves of the tree were for the healing of the nations." The Greek word for "healing" (*therapeian*) is what gives us the term *therapeutic*. John Walvoord notes that the root meaning of the Greek word conveys the idea of "health-giving."[6] There will be no need of healing from sickness or disease because the consequences of sin will have been removed and the "former things are passed away" (21:4 KJV). Thus, the tree and its leaves are seen as a source of life and health in the eternal state.

The ultimate proof that this indeed describes a return to Edenic conditions is the removal of the *divine curse* (Revelation 22:3). This curse was first pronounced against the participants in the first act of rebellion (see Genesis 3:14-19). The actual objects of the curse were Satan and the earth ("ground") itself, but the implications of the curse affected all involved:

- Serpent—cursed above all animals

- Woman—sorrow and pain in childbirth

- Man—"cursed is the ground for your sake"

The Old Testament record of man's rebellion against God begins and ends with a curse. The sin of Adam and Eve is cursed, and its consequences are severe (Genesis 3:14-19). Even in the Law of Moses, there is the threat of the curse for those who break the law (Deuteronomy 27:13-26). And as we just said, the Old Testament ends with the threat of a curse: "...lest I come and smite the earth with a curse" (Malachi 4:6).

The Old Testament begins well ("in the beginning God") and ends badly ("with a curse"). It starts with all the glorious potential of the divine creation and ends with the threat of divine judgment. It opens in paradise and closes with mankind lost in sin's condemnation. How different the New

Testament! It opens with Jesus Christ (Matthew 1:1), and it closes with Jesus Christ (Revelation 22:22). It begins with His first coming and concludes with His second coming.

God Is There!

The removal of the divine curse makes access to God a reality in the new paradise. We are no longer barred from His presence. The throne of God has come to earth and is the central feature of the eternal city. It is the throne of God and the Lamb, who rule jointly over the eternal state. We who believe in Jesus Christ know that He and the Father are one. We believe in Him even though we have never seen Him. But in the eternal city, faith shall become sight—we shall see his face (Revelation 22:4).

The Lord God is all the light we will ever need. Because of God's presence, three things will *not* be found in the new paradise: no night, no candle, and no sun. God will outshine all other light sources because He is the source of light.

We who are seated positionally with Christ in "the heavenly realms" are destined for the throne as joint heirs with Him (Ephesians 1:20; 2:6). In eternity we will continue to reign with Christ "when he hands over the kingdom to God the Father" (1 Corinthians 15:24). Thus, the millennial kingdom will be merged into the eternal kingdom of God forever.

Living with Eternity in Mind

All of us are curious about the future; there is something in human nature that wants to know what is going to happen next. God speaks to that need by revealing the future before it happens. As we have seen in this book, there are many biblical prophecies that give us a picture of the world to come. And that world is one where God is all we will ever need for all eternity.

If we really believe that Jesus Christ is coming again to rapture the church, judge the world, set up His kingdom, and rule for all eternity, then we ought to live like it! Many Christians lose sight of their eternal destiny. They become bogged down with the mundane problems of life and allow themselves to become worried, depressed, angry, or confused. Why? Because they forget what their final destiny is really all about.

If we kept our perspective on eternity, then the problems of earth would not get us down. But the temptation to focus on the temporal instead of the eternal is a constant struggle for all of us. Whether our daily problems revolve around our health, finances, family, friends, career, or temporal security, true Christians must look beyond all of these things to the only real source of security in our lives—Jesus Christ!

Notes

Chapter One—Understanding the Wave

1. Peter Schwartz, *The Art of the Long View* (New York: Doubleday, 1996). Author and president of an international consulting firm, Peter Schwartz presents lessons in thinking for the future. Schwartz offers scenarios from the oil industry that can be applied to all aspects of life. His firsthand accounts, originally developed for Royal Dutch/Shell, are invaluable tools for creative thinking in one's personal life and in business. Schwartz's methods will enable anyone to think more creatively. Liam Fahay has also written a book on future thinking, *Learning from the Future: Competitive Foresight Scenarios* (NY: John Wiley & Sons, 1998). This book reveals how innovative organizations harness imagination and strategic management techniques to create scenarios that simulate future opportunities and threats. Shows how scenario learning readies companies for industry and market evolutions and customers' new needs.

2. James Hendler, article found at wired.com.

3. Article from wired.com.

4. Ibid.

5. Ibid.

6. Ibid.

7. Article by Alex Roland on wired.com.

8. Ibid.

9. Jim Sachs, article from wired.com.

Chapter Two—The Future Is Now

1. Stephen Monsma, *Responsible Technology: A Christian Perspective* (Grand Rapids: Eerdmans, 1986).

2. Ian Barbour, *Ethics in an Age of Technology* (San Francisco: HarperCollins, 1993), p. 3.

3. Ibid

4. Charles Colson, *Against the Night* (Ann Arbor, MI: Servant, 1989), p. 55.

Chapter Three—The Computer Wave

1. From a paper by Alan Turing, "Computing Machinery and Intelligence," published in the journal *Mind*, 1950.

2. James Canton, *Technofutures* (Carlsbad, CA: Hay House, Inc., 1999), p. 5.

3. Ralph Merkle, Xerox.com, 1989.

4. Ibid.

5. Nicholas D'Onofrio, IBM's senior vice president of technology and manufacturing, IBM.com.

6. Neil Gershenfeld, *When Things Start to Think* (New York: Owl Books, 2000), p. 14.

7. Kevin Warwick, "Cyborg 1.0," article that outlines Kevin's plan to become one with his computer, excerpted from wired.com.

Chapter Four—The Global Communications Wave

1. Based on the Oxygen Project website at lcs.mit.edu.

2. Francis Heylighen, *New Scientist* (June 24, 2000).

3. Ibid.

4. Luciano Floridi, "The Future of Organized Knowledge."

5. Michael Arbib

6. Daniel Dennett

7. Excerpted from www.destronfearing.com.

8. Excerpted from www.digitalangel.net/r.htm.

Chapter Five—The Brain Wave—the Future of Education

1. Dr. Stanley Williams article on wired.com.

2. James Canton, *Technofutures* (Carlsbad, CA: Hay House, Inc., 1999), p. 142.

3. Elmer Towns, *Into the Future* (Grand Rapids, MI: Fleming H. Revell, 2000).

Chapter Six—The Biotech Wave

1. John Polkinhorne, "Cloning and the Moral Imperative," in Ronald Cole-Turner, ed. *Human Cloning: Religious Responses* (Louisville: Westminister-John Knox, 1997), p. 42.

2. R. Albert Mohler Jr., "A Brave New World of Cloning: A Christian Worldview Perspective," in Ronald Cole-Turner, ed., *Human Cloning: Religious Responses* (Louisville: Westminister-John Knox, 1997), p. 103.

3. Up-to-the-minute information about the Human Genome Project can be found at www.ornl. gov/TechResources/Human_Genome/home.html.

4. For more information, contact Don Powell, at Sanger Centre, at don@sanger.ac.uk; Seema Kumar, Whitehead Institute, at kumar@wi.mit.edu; Linda Sage, Washington University, at sage@medicine.wustl.edu; Doree Zodrow, Baylor College of Medicine, at sage@medicine. wustl.ed.

5. Francis Collins, Director of the Human Genome Project, "The Charlie Rose Show," #2758, August 29, 2000.

6. Harold Varmus on "The Charlie Rose Show," #R-2709, June 21, 2000, suggested the Human Genome Project will cut 60 percent off the time to produce new treatments. Savio Woo says

two trials of gene therapy have been reported. "The Charlie Rose Show," #2759, August 30, 2000 (repeat of R-2709).

7. Arnold Levine, President, Rockefeller University, "The Charlie Rose Show," #2758, August 29, 2000.

8. Francis Collins, "The Charlie Rose Show," #2758, August 29, 2000. Arguing that the Human Genome Project has attracted the best minds in science, Francis Collins predicts that the treatment of every disease will eventually be affected by this information.

9. Ibid.

10. Richard Young, "The Charlie Rose Show," #2759, August 30, 2000.

11. Ibid.

12. Lawrence Lehman, "The Charlie Rose Show," #2759, August 30, 2000.

13. Leonard Sweet, Auqua Church Group, Loveland, Colorado.

Chapter Nine—The Religion of the Future

1. Elliot Miller, *A Crash Course on the New Age Movement* (Grand Rapids, MI: Baker Book House, 1989), p. 15.

2. Ibid., p. 16.

3. For a general survey of New Age ideas, see the "Spiritual Counterfeits Project" study by Karen Hoyt, *The New Age Rage* (Old Tappan, NJ: Revell, 1987), pp. 21-32.

4. See the insightful survey of transpersonal psychology by William Kilpatric, *The Emperor's New Clothes: The Naked Truth About the New Psychology* (Westchester, IL: Crossway Books, 1985). See also Garth Wood, *The Myth of Neurosis* (New York: Harper & Row, 1986); and Jay Adams, *The Biblical View of Self-Esteem, Self-Love, and Self-Image* (Eugene, OR: Harvest House, 1986).

5. See Dave Hunt and T.A. McMahon, *The Seduction of Christianity* (Eugene, OR: Harvest House, 1985), pp. 77-84.

6. See Teilhard de Chardin, *The Future of Man* (New York: Harper & Row, 1964); *Man's Place in Nature* (London: Collins, 1966); *The Vision of the Past* (New York: Harper & Row, 1966). For an analysis of Chardin's teaching, see N.M. Wildiers, *An Introduction to Teilhard de Chardin* (New York: Harper & Row, 1968); and G.D. Jones, *Teilhard de Chardin: An Analysis and Assessment* (Grand Rapids, MI: Eerdmans, 1969).

7. Teilhard de Chardin, *Hymn of the Universe* (New York: Harper & Row, 1961). He argued that the convergence of all material and psychic forces will eventually combine in an implosion of energy forces.

8. Fritjof Capra, *The Turning Point* (Toronto: Bantam Books, 1982), p. 22.

9. Ibid., p. 302.

10. Miller, p. 65.

11. Donald Keys, *Earth at Omega: Passage to Planetization* (Boston: Branden Press, 1982), p. iv.

12. John White, "Channeling: A Short History of a Long Tradition," *Holistic Life* (Summer 1985), p. 20.

13. Margot Adler, *Drawing Down the Moon* (Boston: Beacon Press, 1979), p. v.

14. Hunt and McMahon, *Seduction of Christianity*, pp. 120-36.

15. Morton Kelsey, *The Christian and the Supernatural* (Minneapolis: Augsburg, 1976), pp. 113-23.

16. Douglas Groothuis, *Unmasking the New Age* (Downers Grove, IL: InterVarsity Press, 1986), pp. 113-23.

17. Shirley MacLaine, *Out on a Limb* (New York: Bantam Books, 1984), p. 236.

18. Ron Rhodes, *The Counterfeit Christ of the New Age Movement* (Grand Rapids, MI: Baker Book House, 1990), pp. 15-18.

19. Ibid., p. 19.

20. Elliot Miller, *A Crash Course on the New Age Movement* (Grand Rapids, MI: Baker Book House, 1989), p. 24.

21. Ibid., pp. 21-22.

22. Marilyn Ferguson, *The Aquarian Conspiracy* (Los Angeles: J.P. Tarcher, 1980). Her claim that there are "legions of conspirators" at every level of government, society, and education is probably overstated but accurately reflects the hopes and dreams of New Age "evangelists."

23. Reproduced and quoted by Constance Cumbey, *The Hidden Dangers of the Rainbow* (Shreveport, LA: Huntington House, 1983), pp. 13-15.

24. Ibid.

25. Miller, p. 197.

26. Ibid., p. 107.

27. Ibid., p. 122.

28. Joe Klimo, *Channeling* (Los Angeles: J.P. Tarcher, 1987), p. 185.

29. Miller, p. 177.

30. Cumbey, p. 7.

Chapter Ten—Globalism and the World Economy

1. Robert Reich, *The Work of Nations* (New York: Alfred Knopf, 1992), p. 3.

2. Quoted by Reich, Ibid., p. 113.

3. Quoted by Reich, Ibid., p. 119.

4. John Naisbitt and Pat Aburdene, *Megatrends 2000* (New York: William Morrow, 1990), p. 39.

5. Ibid., p. 54.

Chapter Eleven—The Struggle for World Dominion

1. Malachi Martin, *The Keys of This Blood: The Struggle for World Dominion Between Pope John Paul II, Mikhail Gorbachev, & the Capitalist West* (New York: Simon & Schuster, 1990).

2. Charles Colson, *Against the Night* (Ann Arbor, MI: Servant Publication, 1989), p. 19.

3. Robert Hughes, "The Fraying of America," *Time*, Feb. 3, 1992, p. 44.

4. Quoted by Hughes, Ibid.

5. Peter Lalonde, *One World Under Antichrist* (Eugene, OR: Harvest House, 1991), pp. 22-24.

6. Ibid., p. 23.

7. George Bush, "Address to the Nation," September 16, 1990.

8. *Time*, Dec. 11, 1989, front cover.

9. Ibid., p. 34.

10. Martin, *The Keys of This Blood*, p. 18.

11. Ibid., p. 117.

12. Henrik Bering-Jensen, "Germany Resurgent," *Insight on the News*, Mar. 23, 1992, p. 7.

13. Ibid., p. 8.

14. Reported in the press, June 8, 1990.

Chapter Twelve—The Coming Tribulation

1. Excerpted from www.destronfearing.com. Their home page has this statement: "Welcome to the Destron Fearing Corporation website. We are excited to bring you information on the following pages that will give you an idea of who we are as an organization and how Destron Fearing fills the important world niche of animal identification.

"We live in a world with over four billion livestock animals and 200 million pets. The need to identify these animals for management, food safety, disease control, and recovery purposes has become more urgent than ever before. The possible applications for visual-identification products, and radio-frequency-identification products, are vast and varied and will continue to grow as the world understands the many practical uses and important benefits ear tag and microchip technology offers."

2. Excerpted from www.templemountfaithful.org, the home page of the Temple Mount and Land of Israel Faithful Movement. The goal of the Temple Mount Faithful is the building of the Third Temple on the Temple Mount in Jerusalem.

3. Excerpted from www.millenniumforum.org. This site will give you insight into the agenda of the Millennium Forum. Their opening statement gives us a picture of their goal to unite the peoples of the world. "We the peoples" are the first three words of the United Nations Charter. They signify that the United Nations, at heart, reflects and represents the highest hopes and aspirations of the peoples of the world.

Chapter Thirteen—The Wave Comes Crashing Down

1. Carroll Quigley, *Tragedy and Hope* (New York: Gsg & Assoc.; 1966).

2. Ibid., p. 950.

3. Ibid.

4. Ibid., p. 132.

5. Ibid.

6. Ibid., p. 323.

7. You can read about this organization at www.bis.org. The BIS fosters the cooperation of central banks and international financial institutions. The BIS does not accept deposits from or generally provide financial services to private individuals or corporate entities.

8. You can read more at www.oecd.org.

9. You can read more about the World Bank at www.worldbank.org. Their mission is to "fight poverty with passion and professionalism for lasting results....To help people help themselves and their environment by providing resources, sharing knowledge, building capacity, and forging partnerships in the public and private sectors....To be an excellent institution able to attract, excite, and nurture diverse and committed staff with exceptional skills who know how to listen and learn."

10. *Time*, Mar. 10, 1980, p. 69.

11. Excerpted from sdnhq.undp.org/about/.

12. Peter Russell, *The Global Brain Awakens* (Palo Alto, CA: Global Brain, 1995).

13. Excerpted from fly.hiwaay.net/~pspoole/echelon.html.

14. Excerpted from www.worldnetdaily.com/bluesky_exnews/19981112_xex_push_hearing.shtml.

Chapter Fourteen—The Millennial Wave

1. *Grant Jeffrey Prophecy Study Bible* (Grand Rapids, MI: Zondervan Publishing House, 1998), pp. 1207-8.

2. Ibid.

3. Tim LaHaye, *Piercing the Future* (Benton, AR: Nelson Walker Publishers, 2000), p. 348.

4. Randall Price, *The Coming Last Days Temple* (Eugene, OR: Harvest House Publishers, 1999), p. 75.

5. Clarence Larkin, *Dispensational Truth* (Philadelphia: Clarence Larkin Publishing, 1918), p. 92.

Chapter Fifteen—Eternity: Beyond the Wave

1. Wilbur Smith, *The Biblical Doctrine of Heaven* (Chicago: Moody Press, 1968), p. 239.

2. Robert Thomas, *Revelation 8–22: An Exegetical Commentary* (Chicago: Moody Press, 1995), p. 442.

3. A.T. Robertson, *Word Pictures in the New Testament* (Grand Rapids, MI: Eerdmans, 1933), Vol. VI, p. 467.

4. G.R. Beasley-Murray, *The Book of Revelation* (London: Marshall, Morgan & Scott, 1978).

5. John MacArthur, *The Glory of Heaven* (Wheaton, IL: Crossway Books, 1996), p. 86.

6. John Walvoord, *The Revelation of Jesus Christ* (Chicago: Moody Press, 1966), p. 330.

Other Good
Harvest House Reading

Earth's Final Hour
Ed Hindson

Going to the heart of today's issues, including miscalculations of Christ's Second Coming, Ed relates them to biblical wisdom and prophecies.

Final Signs
Ed Hindson

Hindson offers fast-moving, intriguing background on more than two dozen of the most amazing prophecies in Scripture, including the move to a world government, the rapture of the church, and the rise of Antichrist and the false prophet.

Is the Antichrist Alive and Well?
Ed Hindson

Casting aside speculation and focusing on biblical scholarship, Dr. Hindson examines the prophecies concerning the Antichrist and points you toward God's Word for the critical discernment you need.

Fast Facts on Bible Prophecy
Thomas Ice and Timothy Demy

An A-to-Z endtimes resource, this book includes more than 175 indepth Bible prophecy definitions, backgrounds, on different interpretations of prophecy, outlines on the timing of prophetic events, and much more.

Jerusalem in Prophecy
Randall Price

Jerusalem has an incredible future in store, and it's at the very center of Bible prophecy. This book reveals what will happen to Jerusalem, who the key players will be, and which signs reveal that we're drawing close.